MUSIC OF ACOMA, ISLETA, COCHITI AND ZUÑI PUEBLOS

Da Capo Press Music Reprint Series

MUSIC OF ACOMA, ISLETA, COCHITI AND ZUÑI PUEBLOS

By Frances Densmore

DA CAPO PRESS · NEW YORK · 1972

Library of Congress Cataloging in Publication Data

Densmore, Frances, 1867-1957.
  Music of Acoma, Isleta, Cochiti, and Zuñi Pueblos.

  (Da Capo Press music reprint series)
  Reprint of the 1957 ed., which was issued as Bulletin
165 of U.S. Bureau of American Ethnology.
  Bibliography: p.
  1. Indians of North America—Music. 2. Pueblo
Indians. I. Title. II. Series: U.S. Bureau of
American Ethnology. Bulletin 165.
ML3557.D3583   1972   784.7'51   72-1877
ISBN 0-306-70505-2

This Da Capo Press edition of *Music of Acoma, Isleta,
Cochiti and Zuñi Pueblos* is an unabridged republication
of the first edition published in Washington, D.C., in
1957 as Bulletin 165 of the Bureau of American Ethnology,
Smithsonian Institution.

Published by Da Capo Press, Inc.
A Subsidiary of Plenum Publishing Corporation
227 West 17th Street, New York, New York 10011

MUSIC OF ACOMA, ISLETA, COCHITI AND ZUÑI PUEBLOS

Acoma singer and informants. *Left to right:* Philip Sanchez, born at Santa Ana Pueblo and adopted at Acoma as an infant; Wilbert Hunt, Acoma; Edward Hunt, Acoma; Mrs. Maria V. Hunt, Acoma; Henry Hunt, Acoma.   Songs were sung by Philip Sanchez and translated by Wilbert Hunt.

SMITHSONIAN INSTITUTION

BUREAU OF AMERICAN ETHNOLOGY

BULLETIN 165

MUSIC OF ACOMA, ISLETA, COCHITI AND ZUÑI PUEBLOS

By

FRANCES DENSMORE

UNITED STATES

GOVERNMENT PRINTING OFFICE

WASHINGTON : 1957

LETTER OF TRANSMITTAL

SMITHSONIAN INSTITUTION,
BUREAU OF AMERICAN ETHNOLOGY,
Washington, D. C., March 1, 1956.
SIR: I have the honor to transmit herewith a manuscript entitled "Music of Acoma, Isleta, Cochiti, and Zuñi Pueblos," by Frances Densmore, and to recommend that it be published as a bulletin of the Bureau of American Ethnology.
Very respectfully yours,

M. W. STIRLING, *Director.*

DR. LEONARD CARMICHAEL,
Secretary, Smithsonian Institution.

FOREWORD

The songs of Pueblo Indians here presented were recorded in 1928, 1930, and 1940, additional translation and information being obtained in 1931 and 1939. The work is essentially musical and the descriptions of various customs are intended as a background for the songs. These descriptions are presented as nearly as possible in the words of the informants.

It was necessary to record Pueblo songs at a low altitude, and grateful acknowledgment is made of the courtesy of Dr. M. W. Stirling, director of the Bureau of American Ethnology, Smithsonian Institution, who made possible the securing of records of Acoma songs by members of that tribe who were in Washington, D. C. Dr. Stirling placed at the writer's disposal the song recordings made for him in 1928, 16 of which are presented (cf. p. 4); also the Acoma portraits (pls. 1, frontispiece; and 2). Acknowledgment is also made of the assistance of Mrs. Phyllis Crandall Connor, director of the Stand Rock Indian Ceremonial at Wisconsin Dells, Wis., who permitted the recording of Isleta, Cochiti, and Zuñi songs by members of those tribes who took part in the ceremonial.

Continuing the former method of analysis, these Pueblo songs are compared in melodic form and rhythm with the songs of Indians living in the north woodland, on the Plains, the high plateau of Utah, the low desert of Arizona, the Northwest coast, and other regions which have previously been studied.[1]

No linguistic study was made, and the native words are generally presented as they were pronounced by the informants.

When recording the songs in Wisconsin the writer had the helpful companionship of her sister Margaret Densmore.

---

[1] See References (Densmore, 1910, 1913, 1918, 1922, 1923, 1926, 1929 a, 1929 b, 1932 a, 1932 b, 1932 c, 1936 a, 1938, 1939, 1943 a, 1943 b, 1956).

CONTENTS

ILLUSTRATIONS

(All plates except frontispiece follow page 118)

PLATES

LIST OF SONGS

1. ARRANGED IN ORDER OF SERIAL NUMBERS

ACOMA—PART 1

SITUI DANCE SONG

CORN DANCE SONGS

HARVEST DANCE SONGS

COMANCHE DANCE SONG

ISLETA

COCHITI

ZUÑI

RAIN DANCE SONG

CORN-GRINDING SONGS

DANCE SONGS

2. ARRANGED IN ORDER OF CATALOG NUMBERS

ACOMA—PART 1

ACOMA—PART 2

Catalog No.	Title of song	Name of singer	Serial No.	Page
1904	Hunting song	Philip Sanchez	17	21
1905	Song concerning the water used in ceremonies.	do	18	22
1906	Mother's song to a baby	do	19	24
1907	Song addressed to medicine bowl	do	20	26
1908	Song during treatment of the sick	do	21	27
1909	A little golden calliste	do	22	30
1910	Winter dance song (a)	do	23	31
1911	Winter dance song (b)	do	24	31
1912	"The rain clouds are caring for the little corn plants."	do	25	33
1913	Opening song of Flower dance	do	26	35
1914	Butterfly song	do	27	36
1915	Flower dance song	do	28	38
1916	Song concerning a visit to other pueblos.	do	29	40
1917	Song addressed to a new chief	do	30	42
1918	"The mockingbird sings in the morning."	do	31	44
1919	"In the west is the home of the raingods."	do	32	46
1920	"The raingods have returned"	do	33	47
1921	"Corn plant, I sing for you"	do	34	48
1922	Song concerning the clouds and fog	do	35	49
1923	Song concerning Laguna Lake	do	36	50
1924	"The sun youth has risen in the east."	do	37	52
1925	"The raingods are coming back"	do	38	54
1926	"The butterfly you painted has flown away."	do	39	56
1927	Song of Comanche dance	do	40	59

ISLETA

Catalog No.	Title of song	Name of singer	Serial No.	Page
1986	Song of Fortynine dance (a)	Anthony Lucero	54	77
1987	Song of Fortynine dance (b)	do	55	78
1988	Song of Fortynine dance (c)	do	56	79
1989	Song to a bee	do	45	67
1990	The sound of the raingods	do	43	64
1991	Corn-grinding song (a)	do	46	68
1992	The coming of the sun	do	41	60
1993	"It is raining"	do	44	66
1994	The sun and the yellow corn	do	42	62
1995	Corn-grinding song (b)	do	47	69
1996	War song (a)	do	48	71
1997	War song (b)	do	49	72
1998	War song (c)	do	50	73

ISLETA—Continued

Catalog No.	Title of song	Name of singer	Serial No.	Page
1999____	First song of Hunci dance_____	Anthony Lucero__	51	74
2000____	Second song of Hunci dance_____	_____do_____	52	75
2001____	Final song of Hunci dance_____	_____do_____	53	76
2002____	Song of the horned toad when putting her children to sleep.	_____do_____	57	80
2003____	"Lady crane, you stole my corn"___	_____do_____	58	81

COCHITI

2004____	Hunting song_____	Evergreen Tree___	66	94
2005____	Buffalo dance song (c)_____	_____do_____	62	86
2006____	Corn dance song_____	_____do_____	64	91
2007____	Ouwe dance song_____	_____do_____	63	88
2008____	Song on evening before the Buffalo dance.	_____do_____	59	83
2009____	Antelope song_____	_____do_____	67	95
2010____	Corn-grinding song_____	_____do_____	65	92
2011____	Buffalo dance song (a)_____	_____do_____	60	84
2012____	Buffalo dance song (b)_____	_____do_____	61	85

ZUÑI

2464____	"The rain is coming"_____	Falling Star_____	68	97
2465____	The mockingbird speaks_____	_____do_____	69	98
2466____	Rain dance song_____	_____do_____	70	99
2467____	The raingods speak_____	_____do_____	71	100
2468____	The badger woman speaks_____	_____do_____	72	101
2469____	At the rainbow spring_____	_____do_____	73	102
2470____	Corn-grinding song (a)_____	_____do_____	74	104
2471____	Corn-grinding song (b)_____	_____do_____	75	105
2472____	Corn-grinding song (c)_____	_____do_____	76	106
2473____	Harvest dance song_____	_____do_____	77	107
2474____	Pleasure dance song (a)_____	_____do_____	78	107
2475____	Pleasure dance song (b)_____	_____do_____	79	108
2476____	Comanche dance song (a)_____	_____do_____	80	109
2477____	Comanche dance song (b)_____	_____do_____	81	110
2478____	Deer dance song_____	_____do_____	82	111

SPECIAL SIGNS USED IN TRANSCRIPTIONS OF SONGS

┌──────────┐ placed above a series of notes indicates that they constitute a rhythmic unit.

The letters A, B, C, and D are used to designate sections, or periods, consisting of a number of measures.

NAMES OF SINGERS [2] AND NUMBER OF SONGS TRANSCRIBED

Philip Sanchez (Acoma songs) _____ 40
Anthony Lucero (Isleta songs) _____ 18
Evergreen Tree (Cochiti songs) _____ 9
Falling Star (Zuñi songs) _____ 15

Total _____ 82

CHARACTERIZATION OF SINGERS

ACOMA

Philip Sanchez (Ho-ni-ya) (pl. 2, *a*) was born at Santa Ana Pueblo and was adopted at Acoma as an infant. He was the only singer who required an interpreter. His songs and information were translated by Wilbert Hunt.

ISLETA

Anthony Lucero (Pawi'tla) (pl. 6, *b*) had been absent from his home in Isleta only a few months when he recorded the songs here presented, and he expected to return home in a short time. He said that his common name is derived from a Spanish word meaning "light" or "brilliant." His native name is Pawi'tla, which was not translated.

COCHITI

Evergreen Tree (Ho'cuke) (pl. 6, *a*) is known by the English translation of his native name. He is a native of Cochiti Pueblo but is familiar with the songs of the entire region. In addition to the Cochiti songs, he recorded songs of the Zuñi, Navaho, and Hopi which were transcribed but are not included in this work. Evergreen Tree has presented Pueblo songs and dances in public exhibitions for many years.

ZUÑI

Falling Star (Mo'yatcun'ne) was born at Zuñi where his father was a singer and dancer. He is also known as Tony Kaäma'si, a name which has no meaning. When about 9 years old he went to the United States Government School at Sante Fe, N. Mex., remaining until he was about 16 years of age. Since that time he has lived in Zuñi and taken part in all the dances, but has never been a leader of the dances. He had never taken part in a public exhibition until 1940 when these songs were recorded, and he expected to return to his quiet life in the Zuñi Pueblo.

INFORMANTS WHO DID NOT RECORD SONGS

ACOMA

Henry Hunt.   Wilbert Hunt.
Mrs. Henry Hunt.   James Paytiamo.

ZUÑI

Margaret Lewis.

---

[2] The native names are being presented in their common English spelling.

MUSIC OF ACOMA, ISLETA, COCHITI, AND ZUÑI PUEBLOS

By FRANCES DENSMORE

THE ACOMA, ISLETA, COCHITI, AND ZUÑI TRIBES

Three linguistic families are represented by the Acoma, Isleta, Cochiti, and Zuñi tribes. The Acoma belong to the western and the Cochiti to the eastern division of the Keresan family, the Isleta belong to the Tanoan and the Zuñi to the Zuñian families.[3]

The native name of the Acoma is Ako'me, meaning "people of the white rock" and their home is on a rock mesa, 357 feet in height, about 60 miles west of the Rio Grande in Valencia County, N. Mex. This has the distinction of being the oldest inhabited settlement in the United States. It is mentioned as early as 1539 by Fray Marcos de Niza and was first visited by members of Coronado's army in the following year. The early Spanish chroniclers estimated its houses at 200, and its warriors at the same number. It is said that as early as 1540 the Acoma were "feared by the whole country round about." They took part in the Pueblo revolt against the Spaniards in 1680, killing their missionary, Fray Lucas Maldonado, "but largely on account of their location and the inaccessibility of their village site, they were not so severely dealt with by the Spaniards as were most of the more easterly pueblos. . . . The Acoma are agriculturists, cultivating by irrigation corn, wheat, calabashes, etc., and raising sheep, goats, cattle and horses. In prehistoric and early historic times they had flocks of domesticated turkeys. They are expert potters but now do little or no weaving."

Isleta is a Tigua pueblo on the west bank of the Rio Grande, about 12 miles south of Albuquerque, N. Mex. The native name of the pueblo is "Shiewhibak" meaning "a knife laid on the ground to play whib." The term "whib" was applied to a native footrace, and the name may have been derived from the location of the old village which was on a narrow delta between the bed of a mountain stream

---

[3] The information on these tribes is quoted or condensed from articles by F. W. Hodge in the Handbook of American Indians (1907, 1910).

1

and the Rio Grande. It was the seat of the Franciscan mission of San Antonio de Isleta prior to 1629. The population of Isleta in 1680 was about 2,000 when the Spanish settlers along the lower Rio Grande took refuge in this pueblo after the uprising that year. Isleta was later abandoned. It is said that the present pueblo was built in 1709 by scattered families of Tigua, gathered by the missionary Juan de la Pena. The population of Isleta was about 1,100 in the early part of the present century.

The Cochiti is a tribe belonging to the eastern branch of the Keresan linguistic family, living on the west bank of the Rio Grande, 27 miles southwest of Santa Fe, N. Mex. They were found living in this location by Oñate in 1596. They "took an active part in the revolt of 1680, but remained in their pueblo for 15 months after the outbreak. . . . . Cochiti was the seat of the Spanish mission of San Bonaventura, with 300 inhabitants in 1680, but it was reduced to a visita of San Domingo after 1782 . . . The Cochiti people occupy a grant of 24,250 acres allotted to them by the Spanish government and confirmed by United States patent in 1854."

Zuñi is the popular name of a Pueblo tribe which constitutes the Zuñian linguistic family. Their home is a permanent pueblo by the same name, on the north bank of the upper Zuñi River in Valencia County, N. Mex., and in summer they also occupy the three neighboring farming villages of Pescado, Nutria, and Ojo Caliente. "The first real information regarding the Zuñi tribe and their seven pueblos was gained by Fray Marcos of Niza, who in 1539 set out . . . to explore the unknown region to the northwest . . . The first Zuñi mission was established at Hawikuh by the Franciscans in the summer of 1629 . . . At the time of the great Pueblo rebellion of 1680 the Zuñi occupied but three towns, excluding Hawikuh." The Zuñi "are quiet, good tempered, and industrious, friendly toward the Americans but jealous and distrustful of the Mexicans and bitter enemies of the Navaho. They adhere tenaciously to their ancient religion, which is closely interwoven with their social organization. . . . In 1910 the population was 1,640."

MUSICAL INSTRUMENTS [4]

The information concerning musical instruments was supplied chiefly by the Acoma. This was not a subject of special inquiry with the Isleta and Cochiti singers, but some data were obtained from the Zuñi singer.

[4] Grateful acknowledgment is made of the courtesy of Dr. Walter Hough, curator of anthropology, U. S. National Museum, who allowed the Acoma to select from the exhibit cases the musical instruments, ceremonial articles, and the ring used on a woman's head when carrying a jar, shown in the accompanying illustrations.

Drums.—The drum used with a majority of Acoma songs is a cylinder with two heads of hide, lashed together with thongs, and is struck with a drumstick having a round, padded end. Philip Sanchez, who recorded the Acoma songs, is seen with a drum which belonged to him (pl. 2, *a*). A larger drum of the same sort is used with the Winter dance. A vase or jar with a cover of white hide (pl. 3, *b*) is used only by a young girl in the Flower dance. The drumstick used with this drum consists of a stick with a large hoop at the end. When in use the lower edge of this hoop is struck upon the drumhead (cf. p. 34). Pounding on a roll of stiff hide is mentioned on page 20, and a unique position of the drum is described on pages 107 and 109. The tapping together of two sticks was substituted for a drum when these songs were recorded.

Flutes.—Each dancer in the Flower dance carries a cane flute. The flute shown in plate 2, *b*, played by Wilbert Hunt, is similar to the Acoma flute.

Rattles.—Two sorts of rattles are used by the Acoma, exclusive of the "scraping sticks" which are classified by the United States National Museum as notched stick rattles. The gourd rattles (pl. 4, *a*) carried by boys in the Flower dance are painted in bright colors. These dancers carry a gourd rattle in the right hand and wear a turtle-shell rattle (pl. 3, *a*) fastened to the right leg below the knee "to mark the time as they dance." Gourd rattles are also used by medicine men when treating the sick.

Notched stick rattles.—This instrument, commonly called scraping sticks, consists of two parts, a stick having notches cut horizontally across its surface and a shorter stick, or a bone, that is rubbed across the notches (pl. 4, *a*). In a typical instrument the notched stick is 20 to 25 inches in length. A sketch of this instrument among the Zuñi, made by Falling Star, shows the notched stick and rubbing stick about the same length, which is unusual. The notched stick is rested on a resonator to amplify the sound, this varying in different localities. The Acoma use a squash for this purpose, the Ute use a shallow basket or a sheet of tin, the Yaqui use a half gourd, and the Papago use an ordinary household basket.

A shallow box was used as a resonator in recording songs that required this accompaniment. This instrument is used by the Acoma with only two dances, one being a "sacred" dance and the other a social dance. The former is the Situi, and the latter was not designated.

The history and distribution of the notched-stick rattle is interesting, the earliest example, so far as known, having been used in Confucian ceremonies in China. It is found in various forms in Japan, Mexico, Guatemala, Puerto Rico, and other countries, and was used by the Negroes in Africa and by the Maya Indians.

ACOMA SONGS

The study of Acoma music was made possible in 1928 by the courtesy of Dr. M. W. Stirling, director of the Bureau of American Ethnology, Smithsonian Institution.

While Dr. Stirling was making ethnological studies with a group of Acoma Indians in Washington, D. C., he had dictaphone records made of 60 of their songs. The actual work of making the recordings was done by Anthony Wilding, Dr. Stirling's assistant. All the songs were sung by Philip Sanchez and interpreted by Wilbert Hunt, this being done prior to the writer's arrival. Dr. Stirling (1942) published the results of his studies with the Acoma in a bulletin of the Bureau of American Ethnology, entitled "Origin Myth of Acoma and Other Records."

The complete group consisted of Edward Hunt (Gi-rri), his wife Maria (Shou-tu-wi), their two sons Henry Hunt (Ki-wa) and Wilbert Hunt (Tse-gi-se-wa), and Philip Sanchez (Ho-ni-ya), who, as stated, was born at Santa Ana Pueblo and adopted as an infant at Acoma (pl. 1, frontispiece).

Dr. Stirling kindly made his recordings available for study, and 16 are included in the present series as part 1. All untranscribed records were studied, and they contained no important peculiarities not in the songs that are presented. Twenty-four Acoma songs were later recorded for the writer and are presented as part 2 (p. 20).

Additional details concerning Acoma songs and customs were obtained in 1931, at Wisconsin Dells, Wis., from James Paytiamo, a cousin of Wilbert Hunt living at Gloriata, N. Mex.

ACOMA SONGS: PART 1

The 16 songs in this section were recorded by Philip Sanchez for Dr. M. W. Stirling and, as stated, are presented with his permission. The class or use of the song is generally indicated by its title.

(Catalog No. 1888)

No. 1. Creation or beginning song

Analysis.—The monotonous introduction which precedes this song is characteristic of pueblo songs and is shown in a majority of the following transcriptions. (Cf. Densmore, 1926, p. 7; and Densmore, 1938, pp. 52 and 183.) A short rhythmic unit occurs throughout the melody and its count divisions are reversed in the 17th and 18th measures. All the tones of the octave except the seventh are present, and the ascending and descending intervals are about equal in number. The repeated portion was sung three times, the transcription being from its third rendition. Slight variations occur in the repetitions of the song, which are not important and cannot be shown in notation.

(Catalog No. 1889)

No. 2. First raingod song

Analysis.—In this melody we have a familiar tone material used in an unfamiliar manner. The tones are those of the fourth 5-toned scale (cf. footnote 1, table 6, p. 115) but the principal interval is a descending fourth. The introductory phrase contains only this interval and is followed by four measures on a major triad. The descending fourth returns in the middle portion of the melody and at its close.

(Catalog No. 1890)

No. 3. Song when setting up Iatiku's altar

Analysis.—This melody contains two peculiarities that occur in other pueblo songs, these being a change of pitch level and a structure that is designated as a period formation. The former has been discussed at length in a previous paper (Densmore, 1938, pp. 52–54, 182, 183). The pitch level is generally raised during the performance but occasionally it is lowered, the change being either a semitone or a whole tone. In some instances the change is affected in a large, ascending interval, the remainder of the performance being on a higher pitch level, but more frequently the change is gradual and extends over a number of measures, after which the new pitch is maintained to the close of the rendition. A singer from Santo Domingo said that his grandfather taught him to raise the pitch during the singing of certain old songs, and Margaret Lewis, a Zuñi informant (cf. pp. 20, 103), said that her people raise the pitch level during the songs for rain but in no other class of songs. An intentional change of pitch level was not discussed with the pueblo singers whose songs are here presented but was noted in the recordings of Acoma, Cochiti, and Zuñi songs. In all instances the transcription is on the pitch of the opening measures. In the Acoma songs the pitch level was raised in Nos. 3, 5, 6, 7, 8, 10, 14, 20, 23, 24, 25, 30, and 39, and lowered in No. 22. In the Isleta songs the pitch was lowered in No. 47. In the Cochiti songs the pitch was raised in No. 66 and lowered in Nos. 62, 63, 65, and 71. Only one song from Zuñi contains a change of pitch, the rendition of No. 73 containing a lowering of pitch, followed by the raising of pitch to the original level (p. 102). The change of pitch varies from less than a semitone to a tone and a half. Several renditions of the present melody were recorded, and at the close of the performance the pitch level was about a semitone higher than at the beginning.

The period formation is a melodic structure that was first noted by the writer in the songs of the Tule Indians of Panama. In clearer form it was found in 38 of 54 Yuman songs (Densmore, 1932 c, pp. 694–700), and in 16 songs of Santo Domingo Pueblo (Densmore, 1938, pp. 52 and 183–184). It occurred in several of the oldest songs of the Choctaw in Mississippi, and in songs of the Cow Creek or northern group of Seminole in Florida by whom they were called "long songs." [5] This structure consists of 2, 3, or occasionally 4 phrases designated as rhythmic periods and marked by the letters *A*, *B*, *C*, and *D*. The second period is usually higher than the first and has a more lively rhythm, especially in its opening measures. In a song containing three periods this characteristic often appears in the third period. There is usually a recurrence of the first period, and slight changes of rhythm may occur throughout the periods. Rhythmic units are indicated in the usual manner and are sometimes different in the several periods, while in other songs the same rhythmic unit usually occurs throughout the melody.

The present song contains two periods, others with this structure being Nos. 4, 5, 7, 8, 11, 13, 14, 17, 19, 21, 24, 25, 26, 29, 33, 34, 35, 36, 41, 48, 50, 51, 53, 54, 55, 56, 65, 66, and 67. The following songs contain three periods: Nos. 22, 23, 27, 28, 30, 37, 38, 39, 42, 43, 44, 45, 46, 47, 49, 59, 62, and 64. The only song containing four periods is No. 39. Thus the present group contains 30 songs with 2 periods, 18 with 3 periods, 1 with 4 periods, and 33 in which this formation does not occur.

This melody contains only the tones of the minor triad and second. The entire song lies above the keynote and its trend is downward.

---

[5] Since the present paper was written, Bur. Amer. Ethnol. Bull. 136, Anthrop. Pap. No. 27, and Bull. 161 have been published. See Densmore, 1943 b and 1956.

(Catalog No. 1891)

No. 4.   Hunter's prayer song

♩ = 96

Fine

Analysis.—Two consecutive descending fourths are the principal intervals in period A of this song. A change of rhythm and a higher pitch appear in the first and second measures of period B, followed by the descending fourths C–G and B-flat–F. The tones are those of the fourth 5-toned scale. Several renditions were recorded and show no change in pitch and only unimportant changes in the melody, these changes probably being due to differences in the words.

(Catalog No. 1892)

No. 5.   Song to the wild animals

♩ = 100
Irregular in tonality

No. 5. Song to the wild animals—Continued

Analysis.—During the four renditions of this song the pitch was raised more than a semitone, the transcription being from the first rendition. The interval of a descending fourth forms the framework of the melody, followed by a descending whole tone. A fourth has been noted as a characteristic interval in songs concerning animals, but the melodic structure of this melody is unusual. Attention is directed to the change of rhythm at the opening of period B, the eighth notes being in groups of three instead of two. The measures in 7–8, 5–8, and 3–8 time occur in all the renditions and probably correspond to the meter of the words. The differences in the renditions are slight and consist in the occasional repetition of a measure or the introduction of an eighth rest for taking breath.

(Catalog No. 1893)

No. 6. Song to the birds

Analysis.—This delightful melody contains the tones of the minor triad and second. The song lies partly above and partly below the keynote and is characterized by the interval of a fourth, frequently noted in songs concerning birds or animals. The semitone is somewhat infrequent in Indian songs but occurs nine times in this melody. A pleasing variety of rhythm is given by the successive eighth notes in contrast to the count division of a 16th followed by a dotted eighth note. The pitch was slightly raised during the repetitions of the song. The repetitions differed in some unimportant note values, but the quarter notes were steadily maintained, giving stability as well as vigor to the melody.

(Catalog No. 1894)

No. 7. Song when going for a drink of medicine

Analysis.—Several renditions of this song were recorded, the performance being about 1 minute in length. During this time the pitch was raised about a whole tone. As in other instances, the transcription is from the first rendition, before the pitch was perceptibly raised. Certain unimportant changes appeared in the note values of period A, in later renditions. The melody is based on the minor triad A–C–E, with a descent to G at the close of the first, second, and last phrases. This is the first song in the present series with a return of period ¾A at its close.

(Catalog No. 1895)

No. 8. Kasewat, matted hair or wig song

Analysis.—In many pueblo songs a rise of pitch extends over a considerable time, but the pitch of this song was raised a semitone during the first 12 measures of the first rendition. It was then raised gradually during the remainder of the performance, so that the entire change was a whole tone during about 1 minute of singing. The pitch is that of the opening measures, and the tones are represented as nearly as is possible in notation. The changes of tempo are frequent, which is unusual. There is an ascent of an octave to the beginning of period B, with its change of rhythm, and a return at the close to the whole-tone progressions which characterized the first period.

(Catalog No. 1896)

No. 9. Song of Brave Man's dance

Analysis.—The keynote is the lowest tone in this song and its prominence is interesting in connection with the title of the song. A similar emphasis on the keynote was found in the songs of Sioux and Chippewa medicine men and seemed to express their confidence in themselves (cf. Densmore, 1918, p. 53). Attention is directed to the rhythmic units of the song and to the triple measures which begin with the same count divisions as the units. The rhythm is somewhat monotonous, suggesting a long continued dance. More than one-third of the intervals are semitones. Ascending and descending intervals are about equal in number.

A song of the Ouwe Dance among the Cochiti is also presented (No. 63).

(Catalog No. 1897)

No. 10. Song of Ouwe dance

Analysis.—The glissando on descending fourths followed by an ascending interval gives a swaying effect to this melody, suggesting the motion of the dance. The melody is framed on a major triad with the fifth as its lowest tone. The pitch level was slightly raised in the repetitions of the song.

The next song is sung during the playing of a game in which a marble is hidden in one of four cylinders, each side of the players, in turn, guessing its location. It was said "if the guessing is correct the marble will be found in the third cylinder." In a description of the hidden-ball game among the Pueblo, by Culin, the tubes are made of wood (Culin, 1907, pp. 357–364, 367–382). In a similar game witnessed among the Papago by the writer, the tubes were made of bamboo reeds (Densmore, 1929 a, pp. 72, 73, 78).

(Catalog No. 1898)

No. 11. Game song

Analysis.—A broad sweep characterizes this melody, in contrast to the game songs of other tribes which are small in compass and simple in progressions. This melody has a compass of 12 tones, spanned by 4 ascending intervals in the 9th and 10th measures. The melody ascends 11 tones by 3 intervals in the fourth and fifth measures. An ascending seventh followed by a descending fifth occurs twice. The tone material is that of the fourth 5-toned scale and the melody lies partly above and partly below the keynote.

(Catalog No. 1899)

No. 12. Agochudi [6] song

Analysis.—The monotonous introduction is particularly long in this melody. The tone material is scanty and consists only of the tones E-flat, B-flat, and C. Their sequence is such as to suggest E-flat as the keynote but the song is classified as irregular in tonality.

---

[6] "Agochudi" is said to be "not a pure Acoma word."

(Catalog No. 1900)

No. 13. Ashiya song

Analysis.—The two periods of this song differ in tempo, rhythm, and melodic structure. The fourth is the most prominent interval in the first period, occurring in several connections. Attention is directed to the consecutive descending fourths in the eighth and ninth measures and to the descending fourths in the succeeding measures. The second period has a compass of only four tones and the rhythm is agitated, with triplets of eighth notes. Several unimportant changes occur in repetitions of the song.

(Catalog No. 1901)

No. 14. Corn-grinding song

Analysis.—The first period of this song has a compass of 11 tones and the second period has a compass of only 5 tones.   In the third and fourth measures the melody descends from its highest to its lowest tone.   No rhythmic unit occurs in this period.   The second period begins with two short phrases that seem to answer one another and are designated as rhythmic units.   These are extended in a third rhythmic unit and varied in the closing measures of the song.   The pitch was raised a semitone during the first rendition, and an additional semitone during the remainder of the performance.   As in other instances, the transcription is on the pitch of the opening measures, the pitch of individual tones being indicated as nearly as is possible in notation.

(Catalog No. 1902)

No. 15. Song telling where maidens are grinding corn

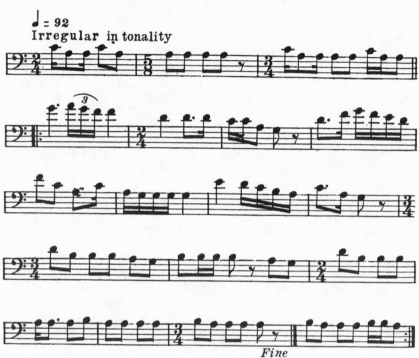

Fine

Analysis.—The dictaphone record of this song comprises the melody with its repeated portions as transcribed, followed by four reptitions of the repeated portion. In some of these repetitions there are slight changes, probably connected with the words, but the triple measure and those that follow are repeated without change. The intervals are somewhat uncertain and the song is classified as irregular in tonality. The rhythm is interesting and the song has an individuality that suggests both pleasure and activity.

(Catalog No. 1903)

No. 16. Deer and antelope song

Analysis.—The most prominent tone in this song is A, yet the melody contains the tones of the fourth 5-toned scale with D as its keynote. The song has a compass of only six tones, but the number of progressions is unusually large. Twenty-six of the 40 intervals are whole tones.

ACOMA SONGS: PART 2

The foregoing songs, as stated, were recorded for Dr. M. W. Stirling, who kindly made them available. The remaining Acoma songs were recorded by the present writer.

HUNTING SONG

The hunting customs of the Acoma center around the possession of a small object called a hunting dog (cf. p. 94). Information on this subject was supplied by James Paytiamo, a native of Acoma, who said the hunting dogs, or fetishes, used by this pueblo were made by prehistoric people and found by the Acoma. They are not natural formations.[7] Every successful hunter has a collection of these hunting dogs, inherited from his ancestors, and when a young man succeeds on the hunt he is presented with one of them. A ceremony accompanies the presentation. If a young man does not receive one as a gift he makes one for himself, hides it and goes to find it, taking a witness with him. A hunting dog acquired in this manner is believed to have the same power as one given ceremonially by an old man, and, it is worn at all times, tied in a corner of the neckkerchief. When a hunter has killed an animal he puts the hunting dog beside it, as though feeding the game to the dog. A prayer is offered at this time.

The hunting song here presented is social in character and would be sung at night, in the camp, when the hunters were getting near the game. Such a song might be composed by the leader of the expedition who would sing it alone, the other hunters dancing. Such songs were sometimes composed by one man and sometimes by two men working together. The accompaniment usually consisted of beating upon a packet of stiff deerhide with a wad of sheephide inside it. The packet was about the size of a small pillow and was laid on the ground. One man beat upon it with an ordinary stick. He knelt beside it on one or both knees, changing his position as might be necessary for his comfort.

When a hunting party returned successful, the leader might start the same song and all the company would sing it with him as they danced.

---

[7] A "hunting dog," or hunting fetish of the Zuñi, was seen in 1939 at Wisconsin Dells, Wis. It was part of a necklace of turquoise and shell owned by Blue Sky from Zuñi, the husband of Margaret Lewis. Blue Sky inherited this necklace from his grandfather. The opportunity to see it was accidental. It had been placed in the noonday sun and the writer chanced to be present when it was brought into the building. Margaret Lewis (pp. 7, 103) said, "Turquoise dies if it is not put in the sun once in a while" and this necklace had been placed in the sun "to give it life." Among the pieces of turquoise was a "hunting dog," recognized at once. It was a natural formation, somewhat oblong in shape with a projection at one corner that suggested a little, pointed head. In this "head" were two tiny black dots, supposed to represent eyes. The size of the piece was about 1 inch by 1½ inches. It was said "when a hunter attended a hunting ceremony he carried such a 'hunting dog' in his bag, together with corn pollen and certain medicines believed to attract animals, especially the deer."

No. 17. Hunting song

(Catalog No. 1904)

Translation

Deer-youth, the one who is four times ahead,
That is the one of whom I am thinking,
It is the kind of robe and the kind of face, the whole body and the kind of health
 he has,
That is the one I am thinking about.
Antelope-youth, the one who is four times ahead,
That is the one of whom I am thinking,
It is the kind of robe and the kind of face, the whole body and the kind of health
 he has,
That is the one I am thinking about.
Somewhere along the edge, under a pine tree,
There you are looking for me, you are waiting for me,
Now I shall follow where you have gone.
Somewhere out on the plain, somewhere among the sages,
There you are looking for me, you are waiting for me,
Now I shall follow where you have gone.

Analysis.—The framework of this song is a major triad with minor seventh added (cf. Nos. 18 and 21). In the first period the tones of the triad occur in descending order. The second period is preceded by an ascent of an octave and its opening measures are framed on the descending tones G-sharp–E–C-sharp –A–E. The song closes on the major triad with the keynote as its highest tone. The principal interval of progression is a fourth.

SONG CONCERNING THE WATER USED IN CEREMONIES

The water used in ceremonies is brought from four directions. The next song is concerning this water and is sung by medicine men as they go in quest of it, also by women as they bring the water to be used ceremonially by the men.

(Catalog No. 1905)

No. 18. Song concerning the water used in ceremonies

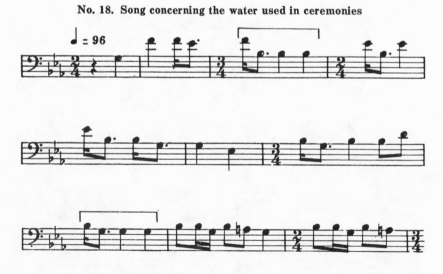

No. 18. Song concerning the water used in ceremonies—Continued

Analysis.—The first period of this song is based on a major triad and the second period is based on the same triad with the minor seventh added, a framework noted in the song next preceding. In several instances these tones occur in unbroken descending order. The minor third between G and B-flat is the most frequent interval in the melody. Next in frequency is the major third which comprises 20 of the 75 progressions. The use of A natural in two measures is interesting, also the ascending seven with which the song begins.

MOTHER'S SONG TO A BABY

In some Acoma families it is the custom to select a baby's name on the fourth night after it is born. Certain songs are sung, and the name for the baby is suggested by the words of these songs. It is said that the songs are "very pretty" and the words are chiefly about the flowers.

A different sort of song is here presented, this being a song that a mother would sing to her baby. It was said "the medicine man is always offering prayers for the little babies and this song tells of the medicine man's prayer through which the baby received life."

(Catalog No. 1906)

No. 19. Mother's song to a baby

No. 19. Mother's song to a baby—Continued

Translation

First, the little baby through the medicine man's prayers has been given life,
Here and there, with the medicine man's song.
For the baby the songs have been sung.
Next, the baby's mother,
With the songs of the rain gods she has cared for the little baby.
Here and there the mother with the cloud cradle,[8]
The little baby was cared for.
It was nice that the clouds came up like foam,
As if it was among those soft little clouds,
With this the baby was cared for.

Analysis.—After a short introduction this song consists of two periods. Each period is major in tonality but has its own keynote. The repetition of the first period shows some rhythmic changes in repeated tones, probably due to a difference in the words. The melody progresses by larger intervals than is usual in Indian songs, about one-third of the intervals being fourths. Next in frequency are major thirds and whole tones.

SONGS CONNECTED WITH TREATMENT OF THE SICK

The healing practice of the Acoma is based on the belief that sickness can be "brushed away."[9] The medicine man who is giving the treatment dances around the sick person and brushes his flesh with eagle feathers, beginning at his head and brushing downward to his feet. The feathers used in the treatment are the longest wing feathers of the eagle, and the medicine man holds two in each hand. Having passed the feathers over the flesh of the sick person, he "knocks the sickness out of the feathers," repeating the action at frequent intervals during the treatment. He has 4 to 10 assisting medicine men, according to the number in his society; they shake gourd rattles and join him in the songs.

---

[8] The "baby carrier," in which a mother carries her baby, is called a cloud cradle.
[9] Information concerning the treatment of the sick was given by Henry Hunt, Mrs. Henry Hunt, Wilbert Hunt, and Philip Sanchez, the entire Acoma group being present only on this occasion.

It is customary for members of all the medicine societies to speak somewhat as follows during the private treatment of the sick:

You can see that I am an ordinary human being. It is a spirit that cures the sick through me. It is not within my power alone but I am taking the place of the spirit that has the power.

Anyone who wishes may "say a few words to encourage the medicine man."

Every medicine man has a dish called *aiwuna yisti* (pl. 5) which he uses in the public treatment of the sick. This treatment is ceremonial in character and many medicine men take part in it, some being actively engaged in the treatment while others sing and shake gourd rattles. The medicine dish (pl. 3, *a*) used in this ceremony is different from the medicine bowl, or dish, mentioned in the song concerning Laguna Lake (No. 36). Into this bowl the medicine man puts a substance made from a snake. He claims that by looking into the bowl he receives clairvoyant power and also is enabled to cure the sick person. The bowl is covered during part of his performance and he removes the cover when desiring to increase his power or knowledge. The use of the "prayer stick" (pl. 3, *a*) was not described.

The following song is used by members of all the societies of medicine men.

(Catalog No. 1907)

No. 20. Song addressed to medicine bowl

Free translation

Medicine bowl, you are going to brush away the sickness

Analysis.—This is a pleasing melody with a simple rhythmic unit and a compass of nine tones. It progresses chiefly by whole tones, which comprise 19 of the 33 intervals. Next in frequency is a minor third. The pitch is raised slightly in repetitions of the song.

There were no words in the song next following, which was sung during the actual treatment of the sick person.

(Catalog No. 1908)

No. 21. Song during treatment of the sick

Analysis.—The framework of this melody consists of the minor triad A–C–E and the major triad F–A–C, the tones of both triads occurring in descending order (cf. analysis of No. 17). The minor third A–C is the continuing interval between these triads and the most frequent interval in the song. No secondary accent occurs in the first and seventh measures which are transcribed in 7–8 time, a secondary accent was, however, given on the fifth count of the third from the final measure. The rhythmic unit is simple and gives steadiness to the melody.

Several consecutive renditions were recorded and show no differences other than the occasional use of an eighth rest as a breathing space and the use of C instead of A in next to the last measure. The drumbeat in quarter notes was heard in the 5–8 and 7–8 measures, the adjustment being by a delay of the beat at the end of these measures. The drum and voice are synchronous at the beginning of the next measures.

A treatment of the eye was described by Mrs. Henry Hunt, who said that she had often been benefited by it and knew of others who had been helped. The treatment was given by a medicine woman in this manner. She cleansed her mouth, chewed a certain medicine, and then put her tongue into the eye of the patient. She sometimes removed foreign bodies from the eyes of her patients. Certain persons made a specialty of this treatment of the eye.

A peculiar importance is given by the Acoma to men who have been struck by lightning. Such men are affiliated, but it does not appear that they constitute one of the medicine men's societies. It is they, and no others, who treat dislocations and fractures.

It was said that when lightning strikes a man he is supposed to be killed but that he will be "put together by the lightning" if another member of the tribe does not see him before the thunder sounds. For this reason the Acoma tell each other not to look at a companion if he is believed to be struck by lightning. They say to each other, "Cover your eyes and turn aside until after you hear the thunder."

A man who has been struck by lightning is considered "initiated." He is taken in charge by a man who has been previously struck by lightning, who guards him for 4 days. During this time the man stays alone and purifies himself with medicine. The members of this group take turns in massaging his whole body, especially his abdomen, and one man of the group adopts him as his son. He is allowed no food during the treatment. On the fourth day he is allowed to eat and go outdoors, and, after performing certain acts, he can treat dislocations, fractures, and similar forms of distress. As a sign of authority he must be able to show the scar made by the lightning on his body.

The man who has taken him as a son goes with him to the place of the accident to search for the flint tip of the lightning bolt. It is the Acoma belief that every bolt of lightning has a flint tip and this, when found, becomes the fetish of the man who was struck by the lightning. When treating a fracture he presses this over the affected part and also uses it in setting a bone.

In his treatment of a fracture, such a man uses a splint from a tree that has been struck by lightning. He binds the broken bone with this splint and leaves it in place until the bone has had time to heal. He then removes the splint and massages the flesh with medicine and replaces the splint. He does not use grease in massaging the fracture, which is the custom among the Sioux and Chippewa (cf. Densmore, 1918, p. 261, and Densmore, 1936 b, pp. 334, 335).

WINTER DANCE SONGS

The Acoma call this the Zuñi dance because it was obtained from that Pueblo, but the Acoma have composed their own songs for it. The dance is also called *Bask*, a term used in no other connection.

Midwinter is the time for this dance which is held in the village plaza. It is a pleasure dance in which many young people take part. There is no special costume, but both young men and girls carry a branch of spruce in each hand, holding it erect as they dance. The girls wear their best raiment, including buckskin sandals and wrappings from ankle to knee; they also wear ceremonial blankets. The singers usually number about 20 and the accompanying instrument is a drum similar to that shown in plate 2, *a*, but larger. One man beats upon it. The dancers form in a double line, two young men being followed by two young girls, who, in turn, are followed by two young men, and so on. The singers and the drummer walk beside them. The entire company moves forward a distance of about 200 feet, then turns and comes back again, the men and girls with a dancing step while the singers walk near them. In dancing this distance they sing four songs without stopping. Occasionally the dancers go back to rest in their chamber.

Four songs comprise a set, as stated, and two songs of a set are presented (Nos. 23, 24). Before singing these songs the singer recorded a song that he designated as "official," though used in a social dance (No. 22). In its original connection this song was sung by a field chief when going out to visit the country and the sheep herders at night. It was part of his duty to protect the tribe by this watchfulness.

(Catalog No. 1909)

No. 22. A little golden calliste

Voice ♩ = 132
Drum ♩ = 132
Drum-rhythm similar to No. 21
Irregular in tonality

Translation

There in the eastern turquoise chamber
There this morning a baby golden calliste (eagle) was born

Analysis.—Two renditions of this song were recorded, the performance lasting about 1½ minutes. During this time the pitch was gradually lowered almost a semitone. The transcription represents the melody as nearly as possible, being on the pitch level of the first rendition. The song is classified as irregular in tonality. The first four measures are chiefly on the descending tones G–E–C–A, followed by six measures suggesting C as their keynote. The principal tones in the second period are C and A, while the closing measures suggest the key of A minor. Attention is directed to the ascent of a ninth between the periods. The drumbeat is synchronous with the voice during the first period, but is indistinct during the second period of the melody.

(Catalog No. 1910)

No. 23. Winter dance song (a)

Analysis.—Like the song next preceding, this contains a change of pitch level but, in contrast to that melody, the pitch is raised. This change is less than a semi-tone in 1½ minutes of performance. The melody is typical of songs on the fourth 5-toned scale except for the use of F in the lower octave. The melody progresses chiefly by whole tones, though the fourth is a prominent interval.

The following is the fourth song of the group, which is always sung immediately before the dancers go back to their chamber for a brief rest.

(Catalog No. 1911)

No. 24. Winter dance song (b)

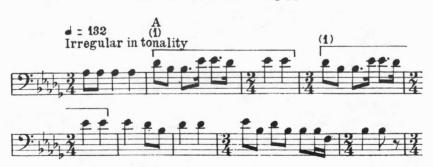

No. 24. Winter dance song (b)—Continued

Analysis.—The renditions of this song occupied 1¼ minutes and the pitch was a semitone higher at the close than at the beginning of the performance. The pitch was raised perceptibly during the first half-minute and the new pitch level was maintained with a fair degree of accuracy. The general trend of the melody suggests the key of B-flat minor but the song is classified as irregular in tonality. The opening measures of period B introduce a new rhythm with a triplet of eighth notes on the unaccented portion of the measure. In the last seven measures the count divisions are reversed, the triplet of eighth notes appearing on the accented beat of the measure.

(Catalog No. 1912)

No. 25. The rain clouds are caring for the little corn plants

Translation

Nicely, nicely, nicely, nicely, there away in the east,
The rain clouds are caring for the little corn plants as a mother takes care of her baby.

Analysis.—In this song the pitch level was raised less than a semitone in 1¼ minutes. The tone material is that of the second 5-toned scale. The structure differs from that of a majority of recorded Acoma songs in that the melody lies entirely above the keynote which occurs as the first and last tones. This is a rhythmic melody yet no phrase can be regarded as a rhythmic unit. Attention is directed to the second measure which is in triple time, and to the fifth and sixth measures which contain the same phrase but are in double time.

FLOWER DANCE SONGS

In February or March of each year the Acoma hold a dance "as an invitation to the flowers to bloom again." This dance is not related to the ceremonies intended to bring rain or secure good crops but is a simple gathering of the people, beginning at sunrise and ending at sunset. Visitors often come from other pueblos to see the dance which is held in the plaza. The Acoma name for this dance is *"gaspirdih,"* a word not used in any other connection.

The most prominent person in this dance is an unmarried girl who may be selected from any family in the village and is usually a girl known to be proficient in the songs and use of the drum. The dancers are 20 unmarried boys, the leader being the boy who first "started to get up the dance," and the next in leadership being the first boy he asked to help make the arrangements.

The girl wears a ceremonial blanket as a robe (pl. 4, *b*), and her hair is arranged in "squash blossoms." The boys wear leggings and moccasins, and their bodies are painted pink without decorative designs. Beads and shells are around their necks and wrists. The sash commonly worn by Acoma women is worn by the boys at this time, being worn over the right shoulder (pl. 4, *b*). Their headdresses are made of artificial flowers and eagle down. The women make the flowers of cloth in all colors and arrange them in a fillet with three tall tufts of eagle down, one above each ear and one in the middle of the front. A replica of this headdress was made by Wilbert Hunt (pl. 5). If a boy has long hair, it is tied in a bunch at the nape of his neck.

The Flower dance is old but only one old song is used, this being the song with which the girl opens the dance. Generally the other songs have been composed since the previous dance, though a song 5 or 6 years old is occasionally used, the words being changed and "the song fixed up a little." There is no formal preparation for the dance, but the boys gather to select and rehearse the songs. They have a meeting place where they gather before the dance and to which they withdraw for the feast at noon, coming and going often to this room during the dance.

When all is ready for the dance, a ceremonial blanket is spread for the girl to kneel upon. She kneels on one knee and beats a vase drum, using a stick with a wide hoop at the end (pl. 3, *b*). The under surface of the hoop strikes the drumhead, the hoop being at right angles to that surface. This vase drum and stick are not used at any other time.

The dancers stand in a line in front of the drum, with their faces toward one end of the line. Each boy has a turtle-shell rattle (pl. 4, *b*) fastened below his right knee, its sound marking the time as he dances.

In his right hand he carries a gourd rattle and in his left hand he has a cane flute.

The girl then sings her song alone. It is short and has no words. At first the drumbeat is slow, then it grows faster and comes to a sudden stop, which is the signal for the boys to join in the singing and begin to dance. The action of the dance consists in a motion of the right foot, upward and downward, and a turning around so that the dancers face in the opposite direction, having the drum alternately at their right and left hand.

(Catalog No. 1913)

No. 26. Opening song of Flower dance

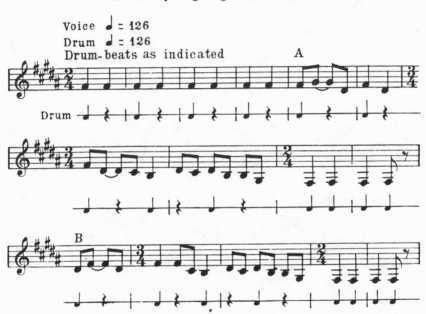

Analysis.—This delightful melody begins with a monotonous introduction. This is followed by two periods of almost equal length, the first having a descent of nine and the second a descent of eight tones. The prolonged tones give an effective swing to the melody, especially when approached by an ascending progression. Attention is directed to the double rhythm of the drum, continuing through the triple measures. The repetitions of the melody are alike in every respect.

Immediately after this song the boys begin a song which they have previously selected and the girl, without singing, beats the drum throughout the rest of the dance. The song of the boys may be one which has been composed since the previous dance, such as the song next following. The first three lines of the words were repeated.

(Catalog No. 1914)

No. 27. Butterfly song

Voice ♩ = 108
Drum and rattle ♩ = 108
Rhythm similar to No. 21

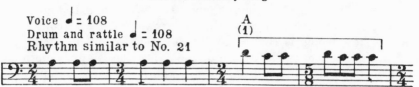

No. 27. Butterfly song—Continued

Translation

Butterfly, butterfly, butterfly, butterfly,
Oh look, see it hovering among the flowers,
It is like a baby trying to walk and not knowing how to go.
The clouds sprinkle down the rain.

Analysis.—Two records of this song were made, the second being chiefly as a record of the drumbeat. This consists of a quarter-note beat in the 2–4 and 3–4 measures, with an additional beat on the fourth count of the 5–8 measures. The drumbeat was clear during almost the entire length of the first record and the beat was the same as in the record made especially for observation of the drum. The form of this melody consists of a short introduction followed by three periods, designated as A, B, and C, the song closing with a repetition of the second period. In this song the third period is the shortest and contains the highest tones.

The next song could be used at any time during the Flower dance. The words were not translated.

(Catalog No. 1915)

No. 28. Flower dance song

No. 28. Flower dance song—Continued

Analysis.—This melody is based on the second 5-toned scale and consists of 3 periods. About one-third of the intervals are larger than a minor third, eight being fourths, an interval often associated with motion. Attention is directed to the drumbeat in the 5–8 and 3–8 measures, being similar to that in the preceding song of the Flower dance.

Just before noon the "country chief" calls from the plaza telling the women to take their gifts of food to the meeting place of the dancers. The women "take nice baskets of food to make the men happy." The Acoma have no fresh fruit and this feast consists of dried fruits and bread, with freshly killed mutton.

The dancers return to the plaza after their noontime feast. A man walks beside the girl, carrying the drum. Everyone sings—the girl, the drum carrier, and the boys—as they return to the plaza. Their song concerns a visit to other pueblos and tells what food they were given. The words with period A were sung twice.

(Catalog No. 1916)

No. 29. Song concerning a visit to other pueblos

Voice ♩ = 69
Drum and rattle ♩ = 69
Rhythm similar to No. 21

Translation

(With period A)

Up from the fish-lake I came out,
When I had come I roamed around,
Then I went away and arrived at Kawai'ik (a Laguna village),
There I arrived, then again I left there,
Then I arrived at Kwiisti village,
There I arrived, and then again I left there and arrived at Tama'ya,
There I spent two nights.
When I left there I came to a cliff and looked down on a village beside a river,
I descended the cliff and arrived at that village—Wi'lapa'ti,
I went up and down the village looking around.

(With period B)

Then my parents [clan relatives] there invited me to a meal,
They invited me to a meal of all kinds of fruit, and I counted mutton, *matchini*
    [thin bread baked on a rock] and a soup made of venison and chili.
Then my parents [clan relatives] there invited me to a meal,
They invited me to a meal of all kinds of fruit, and I counted mutton, *matchini*,
    and a soup made of venison and onions.

Analysis.—In the rhythm of this song we find variations of 1 or 2 simple patterns but no phrase that can be regarded as a rhythmic unit. The tempo is much slower than in the preceding song and the drumbeat is similar to that in other Flower dance songs. Ascending and descending intervals are almost equal in number, the melody containing 38 of the former and 43 of the latter progressions. The song has a compass of 11 tones and is based on the fourth 5-tone scale.

This song is continued until the party reaches the plaza. Everything is then done the same as in the morning, the girl singing her song alone and the boys taking up the singing and beginning to dance at the prescribed signal.

At evening, when the dance is finished, the boys "go and jump in the river to bathe," thus ending the day.

Another Flower dance called the Zuñi Gaspirdih is danced the same as at Zuñi, but the Acoma make their own songs. The action of this dance is like that of the Acoma Winter dance and it is danced in midwinter, in the plaza. Any number of young people, boys and girls, take part in it, the formation consisting of two men followed by two girls who, in turn, are followed by two men, and so on. One drummer and about 20 singers walk beside the dancers who move forward a distance of several hundred feet, then return, with the drummer and singers beside them.

SITUI DANCE SONG

Similar to the raingod dance is the Situi, danced by men who belong to a certain society. This dance is understood only by members of this society but is a source of pleasure to the people. It may be given at any time, winter or summer, either in the plaza during the day or in the kiva at night, and it continues for 1 or 2 days. The songs are accompanied by scraping sticks with squash resonators, played by about 18 women whose faces are covered by yellow masks, like those of the raingods. The funmakers are in evidence, moving among the people, spreading the blankets on which the women musicians are to sit and placing the squash resonators in front of them. The scraping sticks are used with no other sacred dance and with only one secular dance.

The position of the dancers is the same as in the Flower dance and there are several musicians. The men are in a line and face alternately toward the right and left while the women musicians, seated in a line on their blankets, face the dancers. In the words of the next song we find a belief that abundant rain is due to the power of a new chief in an eastern village.

(Catalog No. 1917)

No. 30. Song addressed to a new chief

No. 30. Song addressed to a new chief—Continued

Rhythm of scraping-sticks

Translation

I wonder if somewhere in an eastern village a new chief has arisen for the year,
This is what I said,
I wonder if somewhere in an eastern village a new chief has arisen for the year,
This is what I said.
From the north direction it has rained,
From the west direction the water comes in streams,
In front of the streams of water.
Down toward the east the lightnings come down and strike the earth.
All of us receive life.
Now chief, for this life-giving rain, you must love the earth and the sky.
We all receive the benefit from the rain,
It is the duty of the chief to look after his people,
This is what I ask you to do.
From the south it is raining,
From the east the water is coming in streams,
In front of the streams of water toward the west,
From there westward the lightning strikes the earth,
All of us receive crops.
Now here, chief, are crops.　With this you may love your people.
This I ask of you.

Analysis.—Three records of this interesting song were obtained.   In the first record, from which the transcription was made, the voice was without accompaniment, the second record was accompanied by scraping sticks without a satisfactory resonator, and in the third record a shallow wooden box was used as a resonator. The scraping sticks were crude and intended only to record the sound of the strokes.   This rhythm was in triplets of eighth notes with a downward stroke on the first, a rest on the second, and an upward scraping on the third unit of the triplet.   In portions of the second and third recordings it coincided with the voice.   The first recording comprised two renditions, sung without a pause, the renditions being identical in every respect except the occasional singing of A–E–E instead of A–A–E or the taking of breath in a different measure.   The transcription contains 132 progressions, the most frequent being the major third which occurs 45 times.   Next in frequency is the fourth, occurring 37 times, while the minor third appears only 8 times.   The rise in pitch level is greater than in any other song under analysis, being a tone and a half.

CORN DANCE SONGS

At Acoma Pueblo the Corn dance is called Ya'kahu'na and is said to have originated with the Corn clan.   A group of good singers meet and compose new songs for each season's dance.   Wilbert Hunt said that he had "helped with the Corn dance songs."

The six songs next following may be sung at any time during the Corn dance.   The words of the next song were sung with its second rendition.   In the first rendition a different bird was mentioned but the singer could not identify the bird by its English name.

(Catalog No. 1918)

No. 31. "The mockingbird sings in the morning"

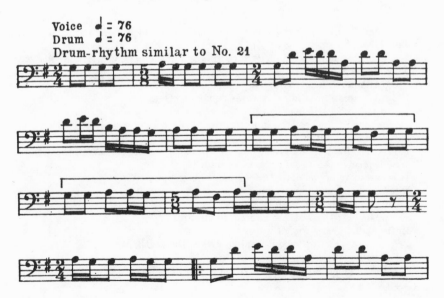

No. 31. "Mockingbird sings in the morning"—Continued

Fine

Translation

The mockingbird, the mockingbird,
In the morning he speaks, in the morning he sings,
For the sake of the people in the morning he speaks,
In the morning he sings

Analysis.—The transcription comprises an introductory phrase of 2 measures followed by a melodic phrase of 10 measures which is repeated with slight changes. It will be noted that the rhythmic unit is a duplication of the introductory phrase with a change of accent. The measures in 3–8 and 5–8 time are usually consecutive, with a quarter-note beat of the drum throughout the two. The count divisions are simple, as in similar songs.

The words of the next song were sung twice.

(Catalog No. 1919)

No. 32. "In the west is the home of the raingods"

Voice ♩ = 88
Drum ♩ = 88
See drum-rhythm below

Drum-rhythm

Translation

There in the west is the home of the raingods,
There in the west is their water pool,
In the middle of the water pool is the spruce tree that they use as a ladder,
Up from the water the raingods draw the crops which give us life,
East from there, on the place where we dance, they lay the crops,
Then up from that place the people receive crops and life.

Analysis.—A count division of eighth notes occurs almost without interruption in this melody. The phrase designated as a rhythmic unit occurs five times and provides a basis for studying the rhythm of the song as a whole. Attention is directed to the measures in double time that begin with the same count divisions as the unit, and to a measure in 7–8 time that resembles the rhythmic unit, also to the final measure which contains a different arrangement of the count divisions which occur in the unit. The song contains 70 intervals, 31 of which are minor thirds and 23 are whole tones, next in frequency being the fourth which occurs 11 times. The melody contains all the tones of the octave except the sixth and has a compass of nine tones.

Concerning the next song it was said "women of the yellow corn clan carry an ear of yellow corn in each hand and make motions with them as they dance." The same is done by women of the blue corn clan, and occasionally white corn is carried in the dance. This song contains many syllables that have no meaning.

(Catalog No. 1920)

No. 33. "The raingods have returned"

Voice ♩ = 168
Drum ♩ = 84
Drum-rhythm similar to No. 21

Fine

Translation

Nicely again the raingods have returned.
Life-giving crops as a gift to the people they have brought.
Nicely again Nawish [a raingod] has arrived,
Rainclouds and game as a gift to the people they have brought,
Nicely the kernels of corn turn yellow,
They form the yellow color.
(Repeated, mentioning blue, then white corn)

Analysis.—This song is less clear in tonality than a majority of the Acoma songs under analysis. The keynote (C) occurs only in the upper register and the third occurs only in the second measure of the song. The principal interval is a whole tone, which comprises about two-thirds of the progressions. The minor third occurs only five times, while the major third and larger intervals are 16 in number. The rhythmic form is clear and contains two rhythmic units.

Attention is directed to the rhythm of the words of the next song, given as nearly as possible in the words of the interpreter and divided according to the cadence of his recitation. The rhythm suggests that of a dance, though different from the rhythm of the melody.

(Catalog No. 1921)

No. 34. "Corn plant, I sing for you"

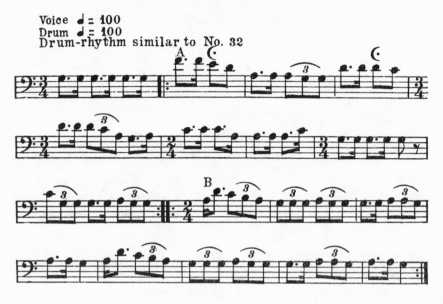

Voice ♩ = 100
Drum ♩ = 100
Drum-rhythm similar to No. 32

Translation

Nicely while it is raining,
Corn plant, I am singing for you,
Nicely while the water is streaming,
Vine plant, I am singing for you.

Analysis.—This melody comprises an introduction and two long periods without the recurrence of the first period which characterizes many of these songs. The same count divisions occur in both periods, but no phrase is indicated as a rhythmic unit. About three-fourths of the progressions are whole tones. The third above the keynote occurs only once and is unaccented, but the sixth occurs frequently. The song is classified as major in tonality.

The words of the following song were not translated but were said to be about the clouds and the fog.

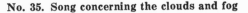

(Catalog No. 1922)

No. 35. Song concerning the clouds and fog

Voice ♩ = 88
Drum ♩ = 88
Drum-rhythm similar to No. 32

Analysis.—This song is characterized by a change of tempo which is maintained for two measures and followed by a return to the original time. These changes are probably connected with the words. The form of the melody is similar to many other Pueblo songs and consists of an introductory phrase and two periods, each of which is repeated. The third above the kenyote is more prominent than in the song next preceding, but the placing of the melody above and below the keynote is the same as in that song. Although groups of four 16th notes occur with frequency, the rhythmic unit is designated as a series of eighth notes in a triple measure. The melody contains a variety of ascending intervals, but the most frequent is the whole tone which comprises almost one-half of the intervals.

In explanation of the next song, used in the Corn dance, it was said there was once a beautiful lake near Laguna which "broke" and the waters drained away. The bowl mentioned in the song is different from the "medicine dish" mentioned in connection with song No. 20.

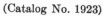

(Catalog No. 1923)

No. 36. Song concerning Laguna Lake

Translation

(Period A)

There was once on the west side of Laguna,
On the lower west side,
A bowl like that in which the medicine man mixes herbs and water,
It used nicely to produce cattails, plants and pollen,
It used nicely to draw the raingods to paint it with sprinkling rain, making
    a picture of the rain.
Now here above us, from the north direction, the duck raingods fly.
They are looking for the medicine bowl west of Laguna.
Alas!   A sad calamity has happened,
Pitiful it is.
Now here about us from the south direction the winter wrens come,
The birds are white and in their flight they look like clouds.
They are looking for the medicine bowl west of Laguna.
Alas!   a sad calamity has happened,
Pitiful it is.

Analysis.—The principal interval in this song is the fourth which is generally associated with birds, animals, or motion in Indian songs.   The interval of a minor third occurs only a few times and is the interval commonly associated with sadness in the usage of the white race.   A short rhythmic unit occurs frequently, also a reversal of the count divisions by which the accent is transferred to the triplet of eighth notes.   The song has a compass of seven tones and is based on the fourth 5-toned scale (cf. footnote 1, table 6, p. 115).

HARVEST DANCE SONGS

The Harvest dance of the Acoma was said to be part of the Corn dance.   Four of its songs were recorded but the customs pertaining to the dance were not a subject of inquiry.   One of the songs, not transcribed, contained these words, the first three lines being sung twice and followed by the last lines which were also repeated.

Look there, somewhere beneath the home of the raingod,
There underneath their home the raingods are painting themselves, with
    their shoes of clouds and with their ceremonial sashes,
With these they look handsome, and now they will return.
This way from the north, from the north path whence I came,
There the old-time prayer-sticks are repainting themselves in the same
    manner.

The three Harvest dance songs here presented were sung with clearness.

(Catalog No. 1924)

No. 37. "The sun-youth has risen in the east"

No. 37. "The sun-youth has risen in the east—Continued

Fine

Translation

There in the east, there in the east,
The sun-youth has risen and has sent out his breath so that the leaves and
all vegetation is in gentle motion.
The sun-youth has risen and has sent out his breath so that the leaves and
all vegetation is in gentle motion,
The corn maidens and the vine maidens are also in motion with this breeze

Analysis.—An introduction and three periods comprise the structure of this
song, the first and second periods being major and the third uncertain in tonality.
The tone transcribed as A-natural in the first period was lower than A-flat but a
somewhat unfocused tone, impossible to indicate in notation. The second period
of the song is higher in pitch and has a different keynote from the first, but the
general character of the melody remains the same. The third period is shorter,
has a rhythm of its own, and is followed by the usual return of a former period
of the song.

(Catalog No. 1925)

No. 38. "The raingods are coming back"

Translation

Yesterday, sometime, somewhere, up from the north
A yellow cloud has set,
Perhaps because the raingods are coming back again
Perhaps because the raingods are coming back again,
The yellow cloud has set.

Yesterday, sometime, somewhere, up from the middle west
A blue cloud has set,
Perhaps because the raingods are coming back again,
Perhaps because the raingods are coming back again,
The blue cloud has set.

This way from the middle direction
Cha-a-ga, a north raingod,
Green corn he has brought for us.
Then go forward, country-chief, carrying with you some prayer-sticks,
Carrying with you prayer-sticks, go forward.

Look there in the snow mountain the rain clouds are coming out,
Then go forward, country-chief, carrying the sticks that the raingods use in
    their stick race,
Carrying also the ring that the women use to hold the water-jar on the head,
Carrying these, go forward,

Look, there is the enchanted mountain,
There the rain clouds are coming up.

Analysis.—This is a florid melody with frequent changes of tempo that probably
correspond to changes in the words.   The melodic form consists of three periods,
the third being short and on the upper tones of the compass, followed by a repetition of the second period.   The first portion of the song is major in tonality with
B as its keynote, and the portion beginning with the change in signature is minor,
with F-sharp as its keynote, the song is therefore classified as both major and
minor in tonality.   About two-thirds of the intervals are whole tones, next in
frequency being fourths and minor thirds.

Philip Sanchez, who recorded the Acoma songs, said that he often
composes songs. He said, "Melodies are always in my mind. I
make up songs when I am by myself, in a sheep camp or such a place."
In some instances the song is developed from a few words and in
others it is suggested by the scenes around him.

He recently painted a butterfly on a small article that he was
making. When he looked at the butterfly, he exclaimed, "It looks
real, as if it could fly away." Then he made this song which he
intends to sing at the Harvest dance on his return to Acoma Pueblo.
The idea of the butterfly and its flight is graceful, but the words do
not contain the high, simple poetry of the old Acoma songs, and their
rhythm, as given by the interpreter, lacks the broad sweep into which
the words of the old songs fall naturally when interpreted. He
requested that the word "chorus" be used.

(Catalog No. 1926)

No. 39. "The butterfly you painted has flown away"

No. 39. "The butterfly you painted has flown away"—Continued

Translation

I

Is it not you, young man, is it not you, young man.
That sort of yellow butterfly you painted,
That flies in among the corn plants.
Is it not you, young man, is it not you, young man,
That sort of blue butterfly you painted,
That flies in among the corn plants.

Chorus

Butterfly, butterfly, that yellow butterfly, that beautiful butterfly [repeated]'
I can see it fly away in its sacred way.

II

Is it not you young man, is it not you, young man?
That kind of yellow butterfly, yellow butterfly you have painted,
So then it is pretty, to alight in the field.

(Repeated, mentioning the blue butterfly)

Chorus

Butterfly, butterfly, yellow, blue butterfly,
Beautiful, beautifully it flies to the country.
Beautiful butterfly, red, white butterfly,
Beautiful, beautifully it has flown among the flowers.

Analysis.—The performance of this song occupied 2 minutes, the entire performance being transcribed. At the close of the repetition of period B, before the half rest, the tone F was sung slightly above the indicated pitch, this rise in pitch level having been gradual. The tone F in the upper octave, occurring early in the fourth period, was clearly sung as F-sharp and the remainder of the performance was on that pitch level. Throughout the observance of a change in pitch level, it has been noted that the change occurs in anticipation of a particularly large interval or, occasionally, in the singing of this unusually large interval. The transcription contains 179 progressions, and the entire performance, including the repeated portions, contains 212 progressions. Although the song is major in tonality, the major third comprises less than 1 percent of the intervals, the melody progressing chiefly by whole tones and semitones. The drumbeat slightly preceded the voice and is in quarter-note values.

COMANCHE DANCE SONG

This is a pleasure dance among the Acoma, but is closely connected with traditions of war (cf. Comanche dance of the Zuñi, p. 109). Only boys and young men take part in the Comanche dance, some appearing like Acoma warriors, while others are in the war regalia of the Plains tribes. It was said, "if wearing a feather bonnet they dance more gracefully and trip along." They carry shields and often dance face to face as though fighting with spears.

The Comanche dance songs used at Acoma are in imitation of songs learned from other tribes. In explanation of the song here presented, it was said that an Acoma was visiting in the north and was told of a devastating battle. "A whole tribe was killed except one boy who started to walk westward. He spoke a few words and then cried for his people. He cried and said that he went west to seek his grave." This was his song.

(Catalog No. 1927)

No. 40. Song of Comanche dance

Voice ♩ = 126
Drum ♩ = 126
Drum-rhythm similar to No. 21

Analysis.—This melody differs from a majority of other Acoma songs in its structure and we note that it was composed in imitation of the songs of another tribe. It contains only the tones of a major triad and sixth, begins on the fifth and ends on the keynote which is approached by an ascending progression. The sixth measure from the close, and the three succeeding measures, contain count divisions like those of the rhythmic unit, but the change from triple to double time transfers the accent. This is an interesting example of thematic treatment.

ISLETA SONGS

The songs of Isleta Pueblo were recorded by Anthony Lucero (pl. 6, *b*), whose native name is Pawi'tla (cf. p. xII). He said the people of Isleta have five "birth clans" and several "worship groups." The birth clans were said to be known as the white, black, yellow, blue, and mixed corn groups. Lucero said further that the tribe is divided into two parts known as "red eyes" (cu'rem) and "black eyes" (ci'funin), and that he belonged to the latter group. The division was a matter of choice, parents allocating their children in one or the other group when they were young. The Isleta are said to have a village chief and 12 subchiefs, 6 from each of the two divisions. The war captains are chosen alternately from these divisions, year by year. Lucero said:

This division goes back to the entrance of the Indians into the world when the Weí'da (Real) Spirit, having created people, sent them on different paths. He stood with arms folded and spoke to one group after another, so that each understood, and said "This is a beautiful world, full of game and with plenty of rain. The rain gods will travel everywhere and take care of you." He spoke to one group which answered "We like that" and then he spoke to the next group. Each understood its instructions and then they went on different paths. Each group has its own ceremonies. Among the instructions given to the Isleta people was the hunting custom and its ceremony. In all the ceremonies it is required that there be the products of nature, such as meat, corn, flowers and shells, to complete the purpose of the ceremony. In summer the desert is in bloom and the medicine men gather the flowers which they dry and powder, ready for ceremonial use in the winter.

CORN-GRINDING SONGS

In the early morning the women at Isleta grind the corn for household use. They sing at their work, and if some of the men are near they may join in the singing. As the women look at the rising sun they think of what may come to their people in the new day. The interpreter said, "The sun brings human lives to the earth and also takes them away. The Great Spirit tells him what to do."

(Catalog No. 1992)

No. 41. The coming of the sun

No. 46. The coming of the sun—Continued

ritard.

Translation

Early this morning the coming of the sun,
For what purpose is it coming?
Perhaps for the cornmeal it is coming.
>Yonder in the west at Shiawibat [10]
>All Isleta maidens, what do you think?
>What do you say?   Shall we sit and sing?

Early this morning the coming of the sun,
For what purpose is it coming?
Perhaps for the yellow dust from the corntassels [pollen] it is coming,
>Yonder in the west at Shiawibat,
>People of Shiawibat, what do you think?
>What do you say?   Shall we sit and sing?

Early this morning the coming of the sun,
For what purpose is it coming?
Perhaps for sons and daughters of the people it is coming.
>Yonder in the west,
>People, what do you think?
>What do you say?   Shall we sit and sing?

[10] The native name of Isleta Pueblo is "Shiewhibak."

Analysis.—The form of this melody is similar to other corn-grinding songs and comprises an introduction and three rhythmic periods, designated as A, B, and C. In this song, period B begins with the same phrase as period A, but soon changes to a rhythm of its own.   The tones are chiefly those of the major triad E-flat–G–B-flat, but a minor third constitutes one-half of the progressions.   With few exceptions this minor third is G–B-flat which forms the pivot of the melody, additional intervals being excursions above or below it.   The keynote is in the lower octave and usually occurs on the unaccented portion of the measure, followed by a rest which seems to give prominence to the tone.

(Catalog No. 1994)

No. 42. The sun and the yellow corn

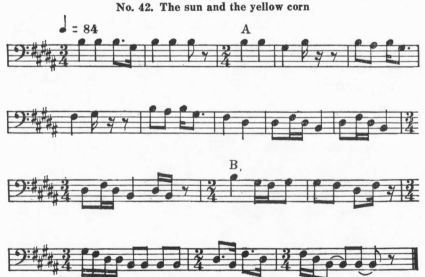

No. 42. The sun and the yellow corn—Continued

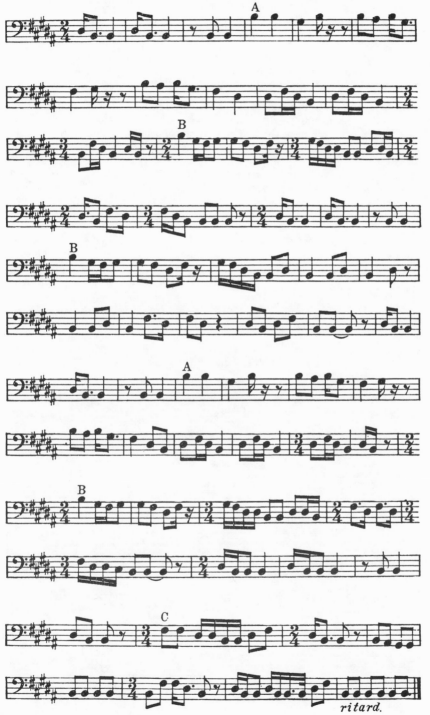

Translation

Over in the east, in the lake of the rising sun (ocean)
Over straight in the east,
The sun and the yellow corn are coming to us.

Over in the east, in the lake of the rising sun,
Over straight in the east,
The sun and the yellow corn are coming among us.

Analysis.—It is impossible to show the structure of this melody without transcribing the entire performance, which is here presented. Attention is directed to a comparison of the four repetitions of section B which are alike only in the first and second measures and in their general rhythm. The three sections marked A are alike in every respect, while section C, as in other corn-grinding songs, occurs only once, and is more lively than the other sections. Major and minor thirds are about equal in number, the former comprising 70 and the latter 78 progressions. The pitch was well maintained and was slightly higher than the transcription.

The word "pretty" occurring in the next song occurs in other translations. It is not used in a trivial sense, but was the nearest English equivalent to the native word. In this, as in other instances, the words chosen by the interpreter are presented in the translations.

(Catalog No. 1990)

No. 43. The sound of the raingods

No. 43. The sound of the raingods—Continued

Translation

How pretty they are coming.
The raingods make a sound up above.
How pretty! How pretty! That is so.
That is why this year the raingods will travel,
How pretty! That is so.
That is why this year the rain will fall,
How pretty! That is so.

Analysis.—The form of this song resembles that of others in the group. It will be noted that period A is based on the minor triad B–D–F-sharp, while periods B and C are based on the major triad D–F-sharp–A, the last period emphasizing each tone of the triad. In structure the song is harmonic, and about three-fourths of the intervals are major and minor thirds. The repeated portions were sung accurately except that the tone A occurring about midway through the song was changed to D when the phrase was repeated. The melody contains all the tones of the octave and has a compass of 13 tones.

The next song contains both Isleta and Hopi words, the latter following the words that were translated. The meaning of the Hopi words was not known.

(Catalog No. 1993)

No. 44. "It is raining"

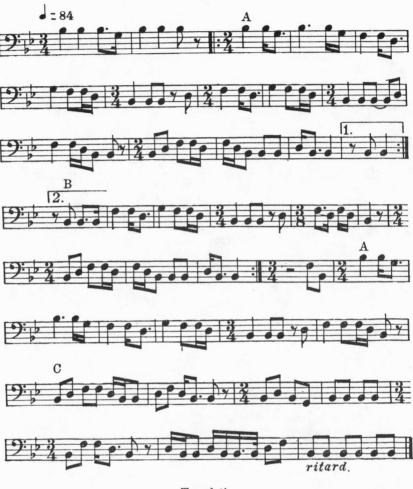

Translation

It is cold.   It is cold.
It is raining.   It is cold.

Analysis.—As in other songs of this group, the transcription shows a complete rendition of the song. The first and second periods are repeated, then follows a partial repetition of the first period and the introduction of the third period which is more lively and ends with the usual repeated tones and ritard. The second measure opens with the same rhythm as the first, but changes to a different rhythm in the second measure. In the repetition of the first period there are two unimportant changes in tones. The most frequent interval is a minor third, although the song is major in tonality. There is a general character throughout the rhythm of the song, but there are few recurrent phrases.

The next song is said to be very old. The native term for bee is *napa* (flower) *juyu'de* (fly). In the song a woman, grinding corn, speaks to the bee. There is undoubtedly a poetry in the words which we miss in the translation.

(Catalog No. 1989)

No. 45. Song to a bee

Translation

Flower-fly, how pretty you sound.
I am very lonely but you sound too far away.

Analysis.—In this and in Nos. 43 and 58 the initial tone is preceded by a short, unaccented tone. An upward toss of the voice precedes the first tone as in a few other songs, but is not clear enough to be indicated in notation. The melody is in the typical form of the series. It is major in tonality, harmonic in structure, and has a compass of 11 tones.

The Isleta have many songs with Hopi, Laguna, and Zuñi words. The next song is an Isleta melody with Hopi words.

(Catalog No. 1991)

No. 46. Corn-grinding song (a)

Translation

How beautiful they are coming

Analysis.—The pitch of the singing was a semitone higher than the transcription, the present signature being used for simplicity. The sprightliness of period C and the ritard in the closing measure are similar to other songs of the group. About two-thirds of the intervals are major and minor thirds.

The next song was composed in Isleta but has Laguna words which were not translated. It is a very old song and is not known in Laguna.

No. 47. Corn-grinding song (b) (Catalog No. 1995)

ritard.

Analysis.—The form of this is the same as the form of other corn-grinding songs, but period B is developed from the latter portion of period A. As in several other songs of the series, there is a slight difference in one measure about midway through period A when it is repeated and also when it follows period B, the same change occurring in both instances. Such changes are not important to the structure of the melody but appear to be intentional and, in this series, occur at about the same point in the phrase, in a measure of somewhat monotonous rhythm. The principal interval is a minor third, next in frequency being major thirds and whole tones.

WAR SONGS

The people at Isleta are said to believe that the spirit of a dead person wanders about and attaches itself to any part of its former body that it is able to reach. Thus the warrior believed that he brought home the spirit of his slain enemy with the scalp. The spirit was not malicious, as among the Papago, who believe that certain illnesses are caused by the spirits of slain Apache (Densmore, 1929 a, pp. 101–114).

Lucero said that his grandfather was a warrior and was one of the men who were "authorized to remove the scalps of the enemy." The method of removing a scalp was therefore known to Lucero, who said the oldtime warriors had an iron implement which they heated and used in burning a line around the entire mass of hair on the enemy's head. The body was laid face downward and little vertical cuts were made in the scalp at the back of the head. The man removing the scalp then "took both hands to it" and "the scalp came off with one pull."

After the warriors returned they tied each scalp at the end of a long pole and carried it in the Scalp dance. It was not inside a hoop at the end of a pole, as among northern tribes; neither was it carried by women. It was said that Pueblo women were kind and domestic and "were not allowed to kill even a bug. If such an act were necessary the woman summoned her husband to perform it." The informant stated, however, that the women at Isleta joined the men in the circle at the Scalp dance. There was a fire in the middle of the circle and, according to available information, the dance seems to have been held near the entrance to the kiva. The songs of this dance were not recorded.

The motion of the Scalp dance was a step forward, then a step backward. The men danced with blankets around them and their arms in any desired position, but the women danced with hands slightly above the level of the elbows and with the palms of the hands held upright and forward. They moved their hands slightly up and down in this position.[11] Seated around the drum were the singers

---

[11] The same position was assumed by women dancers at Neah Bay during the "honor songs." (Cf. Densmore 1939, pl. 21, *a, b, f.*) The writer has not observed the custom in any other tribe.

who might leave the drum and dance if they wished to do so. A
singer wishing to dance was, however, required to go outside the
dance circle and enter it from the outside.

After this dance the scalps were taken to the chief in the kiva,
and the women were not allowed to enter.   The chief took each scalp
and "delivered it to the Great Spirit," saying "So-and-so has brought
home this scalp and has transferred it to me, and I give it to you."
The chief then placed it in a hole in the wall of the kiva, sealing the
hole.   The name of the man who took the scalp was not mentioned
in a song except when the scalp was "walled up."   On a certain
occasion "the chiefs, in a line, go around the edge of the kiva and
one after another knocks on a place where a scalp is walled in.
The wall of the kiva is smooth but the chiefs know where each scalp
was placed."

The warfare of the people at Isleta was chiefly against the Navaho,
so their war songs often contain words ridiculing or taunting the
warriors of that tribe.   For example, a song might say, "The Navaho
came and caught us unprepared but we got our weapons and chased
them two or three days, then we killed and scalped them."

The next song was said to be very old and to be "about a Navaho
spirit."

(Catalog No. 1996)

No. 48. War song (a)

Analysis.—The form of this song resembles that of the corn-grinding songs in its periods and their repetition, but differs in that it contains two instead of three periods and the keynote is the lowest as well as the final tone. Attention is directed to the repetition of the rhythmic unit in period B on tones a fourth lower than in period A. This is the more interesting as both periods are based on the triad above the keynote. Thirteen of the 65 intervals are fourths and more than half are whole tones. The rhythmic unit is a detached phrase, having no influence on the rhythm of the song as a whole. The pitch at the close of period A was a semitone lower than at the beginning. This lowering of pitch was not gradual. The tone transcribed as E-flat at the end of the period was sung a semitone lower than the indicated pitch and in the succeeding measures it was slightly raised, though returning to the lower pitch at the close of the song. The singer recorded a repetition of this song after a short pause. This repetition began on D and sank to D-flat by the end of the first period, ending on the lower pitch. The measures in 3–8 time were uniform in the two renditions.

It was said that the next song is an old melody to which new words could be added if desired.

(Catalog No. 1997)

No. 49. War song (b)

Analysis.—In this, as in the song next preceding, the entire melody lies above the keynote. The first period occurs only at the beginning of the song, differing from several other songs in which it occurs also at the close. All the tones of the octave except the seventh are present in the melody, which is harmonic in structure.

(Catalog No. 1998)

No. 50. War song (c)

Analysis.—This song was sung in the Scalp dance and every phrase expresses joy and excitement. The rhythmic unit is short and clear cut, ending with a downward progression. About half the intervals are whole tones, next in frequency being the fourth which occurs equally in ascending and descending progression.

HUNCI DANCE SONGS

Three songs of a social dance called "hu'nci" (also "hunco") were recorded. The meaning of the name is not known. The dance may be held at any time, either in a house or in the community hall. If held in a house, it is by invitation; if in the community hall, it is attended by anyone who wishes to go. At a small dance there may be only two singers, and at a large dance there are never more than four singers. Either a hand drum or a double-headed drum is used by each singer. Persons sitting near the drummers may join in the singing if they wish. The drumbeat was not always clear and is not indicated in the transcriptions. In the first song the beat consisted of approximate quarter notes, each preceded by a short unaccented stroke. In the other songs this preliminary stroke was omitted.

Both men and women take part in this dance. At first they stand in two lines facing each other, the men in one line and the women in the other, while this song is sung.

(Catalog No. 1999)

No. 51. First song of Hunci dance

Analysis.—The rhythm of this song is unusual and interesting. The melody is based on the fourth 5-toned scale and lies partly above and partly below the keynote.

During the next song the dancing begins and the tempo of the music increases. Each man puts his hands on the shoulders of the woman

opposite and dances around her. She "does a dance step" as she
turns, but does not change her position. If desired, she may dance
around the man in a similar manner, moving in the reverse direction.

(Catalog No. 2000)

No. 52. Second song of Hunci dance

Fine

Analysis.—Although a rhythmic unit is indicated in this transcription, the
principal rhythm is that of the melody as a whole. Attention is directed to a
comparison between the two measures following the rhythmic unit and the two
measures at the close of the song, these differing only in the division of one
count. The song is minor in tonality and contains all the tones of the octave
except the second and seventh. The tempo was gradually increased from
♩=104 to ♩=126 during the rendition of the song, this change being customary
in the dance. During this increase of tempo the preliminary drumbeat was
discontinued.

During the next song each dancer places his (or her) hands on the
elbows of the opposite dancer and sways both arms and body in a
graceful motion. The same position was seen in a dance of the
Papago at San Xavier, Ariz., which was called the Mexican dance.
Couples face one another with arms similarly placed as in the Friend-
ship dance of the Menominee and Winnebago in Wisconsin, but in
the former tribe the dance resembles a slow waltz while in the latter
tribe the motion may vary according to the wishes of the dancers.[12]

---

[12] Concerning the dance among the Menominee, cf. Densmore (1932 a, p. 194). The Winnebago dance
is described and 2 of its songs presented in unpublished material on the tribe, in possession of the Bureau
of American Ethnology (Densmore, MS.)

(Catalog No. 2001)

No. 53. Final song of Hunci dance

Analysis.—This interesting melody is based on the fourth 5-toned scale. It is a lively song, yet possesses dignity and a certain plaintive quality. Like many other Pueblo songs it is in two sections, each having its own rhythm. The first is major in tonality and positive in character, with accented quarter notes, while the second is minor in tonality, with accented eighth notes, and a descending trend in each phrase.

FORTYNINE DANCE SONGS

This was said to be an old dance that is no longer danced at Isleta. It is widely used among tribes of the Plains, and was witnessed among the Winnebago and Menominee, five of the Winnebago songs being recorded (Densmore, MS.). In both tribes it was said that the name of the dance was derived from that of the regiment in which certain Indians served in World War I. It appears to be a very old social dance that has become associated with war.

At Isleta, the drummer usually led the singing. He started the songs and anyone who wished to join was at liberty to do so.

(Catalog No. 1986)

No. 54. Song of Fortynine dance (a)

Voice ♩ = 112
Drum ♩ = 112
Drum-rhythm similar to No. 30

Analysis.—The thematic structure of this melody is unusually interesting. In the first measure of period B we have a reversal of the count divisions in the first measure of period A. In the rhythmic unit we have the first measure of period A with an additional count, this unit being followed by a repetition of period B in the lower octave. It is impossible to indicate with exactness the pitch of the lower tones in the rhythmic unit as they were sung with what may be termed a *dip* of the voice. The song has the large compass of 13 tones and the outermost tones of the compass were clearly sung. Three renditions were recorded, the song being repeated in each rendition. The pitch and the repetitions of tones are alike, except that the connective measures on a single tone at the close of period A were prolonged in the second rendition.

(Catalog No. 1987)

No. 55. Song of Fortynine dance (b)

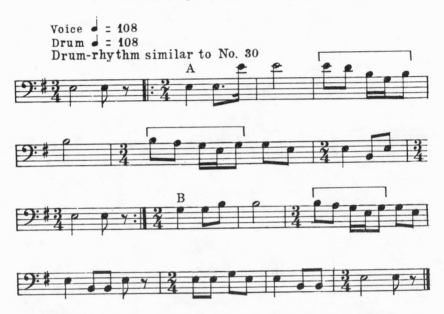

Analysis.—The first period of this song contains a descent of 11 tones, the first descent being a sixth, followed by a minor triad and a repetition of the fourth in the lower octave. The second period of the melody is based on the minor triad followed by a descending fourth. This period of the melody resembles the first without being an exact repetition. The song was sung twice with a pause between the renditions.

(Catalog No. 1988)

No. 56. Song of Fortynine dance (c)

Voice ♩ = 104
Drum ♩ = 104
Drum-rhythm
similar to No. 54

Analysis.—Two rhythmic units occur in this song. The first rhythmic unit occurs in both double and triple measures in the opening period and is repeated near the close of the song. The second rhythmic unit is long and occurs only in the second period. The descending 16th notes in this unit were sung with a sliding of the voice which cannot be shown in notation. The song is based on the second (minor) 5-toned scale, is harmonic in structure, and has a compass of 11 tones. It has an interesting rhythmic effect when sung as transcribed, with the two endings. Two renditions were recorded and show no differences.

SONGS FOR CHILDREN

Two songs for children are here presented. Lucero said that his mother sang them to him when he was a child, to put him to sleep.

The first song of the group was said to be the song with which the horned toad put her children to sleep. It was said "the song has no words because the horned toad cannot talk." The records of both songs are slower and softer at the close, this being the customary manner of singing the songs.

(Catalog No. 2002)

No. 57. Song of the horned toad when putting her children to sleep

Analysis.—The chief interest of this melody lies in the treatment of the rhythmic unit. After two occurrences the second measure of the unit is changed from double to triple time, thus changing the accent on a quarter note. The melody contains the tones of the fourth (major) 5-toned scale and has a generally descending trend. The opening phrase is based on the descending tetrachords E–D–B, D–B–A, and A–G–D. The fifth above the keynote is a particularly prominent tone, occurring in both the upper and lower octaves.

In the next song a woman sings to her child about a situation that would be familiar to the little listener. A crane has stolen some corn. The sound supposed to be made by the departing crane is heard in the first four measures and at the close, this being a syllable resembling *tui, tui* on the quarter notes with shorter syllables on the shorter tones. The words occur with the descending phrases, which have a beseeching quality. These phrases have the same compass but each is in a different rhythm.

(Catalog No. 2003)

No. 58. "Lady crane, you stole my corn"

Translation

Lady crane, you stole my corn
Three bags of it

Analysis.—A slight lingering on each of the repeated quarter notes is an interesting peculiarity of this song and is in contrast to the descending phrases which were sung crisply. The principal melody tones are B, G, and D, usually in descending order, and the intervals comprise 12 ascending and 13 descending progressions. The ritard at the close is similar to that in the song next preceding.

Several Isleta songs recorded by Lucero were not transcribed, among them being a hunting song. In explanation, Lucero said the principal game hunted by the people at Isleta is the rabbit. In former times the weapons were clubs, bows and arrows, and the hunt is still held on three Sundays in May. On the night before each hunt the Indians build a bonfire and sit around it. The singers consist of the war captains and certain other members of the tribe who take turns in beating the drum during two or more songs. The drum is the same that is used in ceremonies and is a tall, double-headed drum, struck with the hands. The hunting songs have no prescribed order.

After singing around the bonfire they go to the house of the animal clan and "have a ceremony" which any member of the tribe may attend. A little altar is made and "they have a painting and certain images." The chief and his assistant "use sacred flowers in the ceremony." They also "burn the feet of the animals they are going to hunt, so the animals will be weak and cannot travel far."

The next day they go out and make a great circle around the game. It is said the animals seem powerless and sometimes run toward the hunters.

Each man keeps the rabbits that he kills and discards the hide, drying the meat or using it in any way he desires.

COCHITI SONGS

The songs of Cochiti Pueblo were recorded by Evergreen Tree (pl. 6, *b*), a man from that pueblo (cf. Characterization of singers, p. XII). The records were made in 1930 at Wisconsin Dells, Wis., and he gave additional information and translations in 1931 and 1939. The place of recording the songs was picturesque. Evergreen Tree consented to sing on condition that the songs be recorded under a little arbor he had made near the house of a friend. The arbor was surrounded by vines, and above were the overhanging branches of trees. Against one tree he had placed a short ladder, which remotely suggested the pueblo. In this arbor he spent much of his leisure time. The place was safe from intrusion but not adapted to sound recording and the records were difficult to transcribe. The recording instrument was a dictaphone with storage battery. It would have been impossible to use a phonograph under these conditions.

BUFFALO DANCE SONGS

The buffalo hunt of the Cochiti was held in summer and took the Indians to the plains of eastern New Mexico (cf. Benedict, 1931, pp. 197–200). This was not like an ordinary hunting expedition, for the people held the buffalo in high esteem, saying "the buffalo never turns to right or left but always moves forward." The hunt was preceded by a dance that lasted only 1 day, and its purpose was to honor the buffalo "who gave his flesh for the good of the people."

On the evening before the Buffalo dance there was an announcement of the event by the dancers from both kivas. This was called by a term literally translated "taking out the rooster." Members of each kiva group met in their respective community houses. According to this informant, the Cochiti clans are Sun, Water, Cottonwood, Oak, Corn, Fire, Turquoise, Calabash, Bear, Coyote, and Mountain lion. He belonged to the Calabash clan which had its community house on the west side of the plaza. The Turquoise was one of the clans on the east side of the plaza. In announcing the Buffalo dance, one group, with many drummers, went around the plaza singing and dancing, then returned to their community house. Then the other group did the same, but did not give the same dance. Remembering the scene, Evergreen Tree said, "it was dusk when the singers went through the streets and they could see the women in the houses getting the food ready for the feast. At about 9 o'clock they were putting the pumpkins in the ovens to bake. In the morning they would take them out, steaming hot."

The following song was sung by one of these groups of dancers.

(Catalog No. 2008)

No. 59. Song on evening before the buffalo dance

Analysis.—This pleasing and simple melody is major in tonality and consists of two sections, or periods, each with its own rhythm. The song is based on a major triad but the fourth is a prominent interval. The low tone at the close of the transcription was below the natural range of the singer's voice but was audible.

When the Buffalo dance is given in the pueblo the company includes a man called the "buffalo bringer," two men who represent buffalo, and a woman called the "buffalo maiden." The dancers enter the plaza led by the "buffalo bringer," who dances with a peculiar step. Behind him comes the "first buffalo," followed by the "buffalo maiden." There are no special requirements for the last-named part, but it is usually taken by a woman who has taken it before and is familiar with the procedure. She is followed by the "second buffalo." Both men who represent buffalo carry a small gourd rattle in one hand and a feathered bamboo rod in the other hand. This rod is about 3 feet in length, and decorated with four eagle feathers, one at the top and the others equidistant to the man's hand. These men imitate the buffalo in their actions. Beside this little procession are 6 or 8 drummers and singers with many dancers. The drum carried in this procession is the usual double-headed drum of the Pueblo Indians.

The Buffalo dance is still given at Cochiti Pueblo, but its significance is gone. It was given by a small group of Pueblo Indians at Wisconsin Dells in 1930 and witnessed by the writer, Evergreen Tree being one of the dancers. The songs of the Buffalo dance are very old and the syllables now sung with these songs are probably parts of obsolete words whose meaning has been forgotten.

(Catalog No. 2011)

No. 60. Buffalo Dance song (a)

Analysis.—Three separate renditions of this song were recorded, the transcription being from the second rendition. The renditions differ only in the order of a few unimportant progressions. In the first rendition the drumbeat was in quarter notes. The second and third renditions were preceded by drumming in 16th-note values, this introductory drumming being equivalent in time to one complete measure and the incomplete part of the first measure in the transcription. The drum was silent during the rests in the song. Five rhythmic units are indicated. The reversals of the count divisions are interesting and give coherence to the rhythm of the melody as a whole. The song has a compass of six tones and is based on the fourth 5-toned scale.

No. 61. Buffalo Dance song (b)

Analysis.—This melody is interesting in its use of both D-natural and D-sharp, each being sung distinctly. It will be noted that the opening measures are based on a descending major third, while the second period opens with a minor third and the descending fourth E–B, followed in the next measure by D–A, the song closing with the descending fourth A–E. This melodic form is unusual. The preliminary drumming was similar to that in the song next preceding.

(Catalog No. 2005)

No. 62. Buffalo Dance song (c)

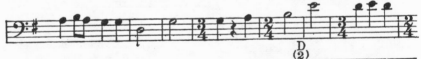

No. 62. Buffalo Dance song (c)—Continued

Analysis.—This song was difficult to transcribe as the pitch was lowered a semi-tone and the time increased suddenly, then increased gradually as indicated. The pitch was gradually lowered while the tempo was increasing. This is not shown in the transcription which is on the original pitch. A slight lowering of pitch level was heard in some other renditions by this singer. He stated, however, that he was not aware of such a custom among the Cochiti. He learned many songs from his grandfather and it is possible that he learned them with a lowering of pitch and did not realize it was intentional.

OUWE DANCE SONGS

In February, before there is any planting, the Cochiti dance the Ouwe dance in order that they may have good crops. Each kiva group has its own songs and rehearses them for several weeks before the dance. The costumes are elaborate and the dancing begins about 9 o'clock in the evening, continuing until 3 or 4 o'clock in the morning. Four times during the night the people and singers from the Squash kiva visit the Turquoise kiva and sing, the visit being returned by members of the Turquoise group. In the dance of the Squash people the men are in the front line and the women behind them. A man with a drum stands still in front of the dancers. The songs mention every sort of vegetable and ask for an abundance of each.

The following song, like others recorded by Evergreen Tree, was used by Indians belonging to the Squash kiva, and he demonstrated the gestures that were taught him by his father. These were in the nature of a pantomime concerning the subject of the song and accompanied the singing.

(Catalog No. 2007)

No. 63. Ouwe dance song

No. 63. Ouwe dance song—Continued

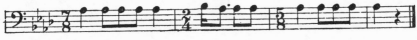

Translation

(Section A)

They go on, on, on, on,
In the early morning, speaking, singing,
There they come by the sacred spring with the rain-boy, while the rain-spirits sing.
We hear this while we listen and it makes our hearts happy,
And out in the great open the people and crops rejoice, for it is for our sakes they have come, and it makes us sing.

(Section B)

Early this morning the happy rain-boy came forth to meet the chief of the warriors, to beckon him to this happy gathering,
While the young maidens join them, happily dancing as other members look on.
Then the rain-spirits also come and form themselves above, and the earth-sign [13] appears in the skies and comes down to alight.

(Section C)

They descend and then go onward.

Analysis.—Each section, or period, of this song has its own rythm and rythmic unit as well as its own words. The pitch was lowered a semitone during one rendition, the change being most rapid in the third period. In other renditions the change was so gradual that it was scarcely perceptible, but at the end of nine measures the lower pitch was established, and was maintained to the close of the performance. Attention is directed to the change of tempo during this period. The general count divisions are the same in all the periods, but their arrangement is different. Thus the third period contains a reversal of the count divisions in the second period. The interval of a whole tone occurs 72 times and a minor third occurs 21 times, the interval next in frequency being a major third which occurs only 14 times. The song is minor in tonality and has a compass of an octave.

CORN DANCE SONGS

Each pueblo holds its Corn dance on the name day of its patron saint, and the Cochiti hold theirs on Saint Bonaventure's day, which is July 14. Each kiva group has its own songs for this, as for other dances, and rehearses them for several weeks. The pantomine, or gestures accompanying the songs, represents the growing of the corn and other vegetables and the coming of the clouds and rain. The words of the next song mention the yellow and blue corn. A repetition of the song would have mentioned the red and white corn.

---

[13] According to this informant, the "earth-sign" represented clouds and consisted of a few "steps" descending and then ascending. Reversed, with the "steps" ascending and then descending, it was said to represent the "earth altar."

(Catalog No. 2006)

No. 64. Corn Dance song

Translation

(Section A)

Come, let us go,
Yellow and blue, as you come to meet one another,
We go right on, we go right up and out into the open spaces.

(Sections B and C, designated as a "chorus")

My dears, my dears, you yellow corn maidens,
As you rise up I see you,
Then I sing for you.

Analysis.—This melody consists of three sections, or periods, the first and second being repeated. The third period has the same rhythmic unit as the second. The principal intervals and whole tones, minor thirds and fourths, with frequency in the above order. The rhythmic unit is crisp and the melody is lively, the changes in tempo probably corresponding to the words of the song.

CORN-GRINDING SONGS

The Cochiti song of grinding corn is that of the preparation of corn for household use (Benedict, 1931, pp. 14, 15). Similar songs from other pueblos are presented (Nos. 14, 15, 41–47, and 74–76). The grinding of corn for ceremonial use in Santo Domingo Pueblo was accompanied by the playing of flutes (Densmore, 1938, pp. 112–119).

It was said that no color of corn except blue was mentioned in the next song.

(Catalog No. 2010)

No. 65. Corn-grinding song

No. 65. Corn-grinding song—Continued

Translation

Great sun, great sun, look down on us children and on the mothers and young maidens while they toil grinding our sacred blue corn.

Analysis.—This song is transcribed on the pitch of the opening measures. The pitch was lowered gradually during period A and was found to be a semitone lower in the second measure of period B, this pitch being maintained to the close of the performance. The song is harmonic in structure and contains only the tones of the major triad and sixth. The interval of a major third comprises 36 of the 75 progressions, while the interval of a fourth occurs only four times. The rapid tones in the first ending were not sung in exact time, the transcription representing them as nearly as possible. Each period has its own rhythm, and there is no phrase that can be designated as a rhythmic unit.

HUNTING SONGS

In old times the Cochiti hunted the antelope and deer, and occasionally the elk and bear, in addition to the buffalo. (Cf. description of an antelope hunter who disguised himself as an antelope (Benedict, 1931, p. 200).)

On the evening before their departure the hunters sat around a fire of logs and discussed their plans. They talked of the places where they intended to go and the game they expected to secure. Each man had his "hunting medicine" in which he placed the greatest confidence. As in other pueblos, the "hunting fetish" was a small representation of a bird or animal (cf. p. 20). Evergreen Tree said this was generally made of soft stone, carved or "worked" with harder stone, and was occasionally made of clay, but a natural formation of stone suggesting the shape of an animal was considered more powerful. If the hunter was an ordinary member of the tribe, he carried his fetish in a pouch at his belt with cornmeal around it, but if he belonged to one of the "sacred groups" he might place corn pollen with the fetish. He said the groups which used the corn pollen were the "Flint, Giant and Herb groups."

As the men sat around the fire they sang songs addressed to the spirits that give success to hunters. Anyone who knew the songs could join in the singing. The song which follows is very old and words occur only with the first portion of the melody.

(Catalog No. 2004)

No. 66. Hunting song

Translation

The deer, the deer, here he went,
Here are his tracks over mother earth, mother earth,
Tramping, tramping through the deep forest with none to disturb him from
above or below.

Analysis.—The pitch was raised a semitone during the first seven measures
of this song, the higher pitch being maintained to the end of the performance.
Two rhythmic units are indicated, though the phrases differ in only one count.
Closely resembling these are two measures before the second rhythmic unit and
the third and fourth measures of the repeated portion. The song lies entirely
below the keynote, which is unusual. Almost half the intervals are semitones,
occurring chiefly in descending progression, but a majority of the phrases end
with an ascending semitone.

The next song was never sung with a drum, the only accompanying
instrument being a gourd rattle. No information was obtained concerning this hunting song.

(Catalog No. 2009)

No. 67. Antelope song

No. 67. Antelope song—Continued

Analysis.—The pitch was maintained throughout this melody though the unusual interval of an ascending 12th occurs between the periods. The song has a compass of 13 tones and is major in tonality, with strongly accented tones that are unusual in Indian songs. It is impossible to transcribe in full the exclamatory phrases at the end of this song, the indicated tones being repeated many times. It is a lively melody, containing 46 measures and 104 intervals, and the progressions are larger than in a majority of Indian songs, more than half the progressions being larger than a minor third. Twenty-five of the intervals are fourths, which occur about equally in ascending and descending progression. This interval appears in the opening measures as the descending interval B–F-sharp, then as C-sharp–G-sharp, and later as F-sharp–C-sharp in the upper octave. A major triad is prominent in the closing measures.

ZUÑI SONGS

RAIN DANCE SONGS

The Rain dance songs here presented are those of lay participants in the dance. Falling Star, who recorded the Zuñi songs, has thus taken part in the dance for many years. (Cf. Characterization of Singers, p. XII.) The explanations and the translations of the words are presented in his own simple language. According to Falling Star, the priests are in the kiva praying for rain during 4 or 8 days. Meantime the men dance in the plaza "to help the priests." Their dancing is in charge of certain men, but all who wish to take part in the dancing may do so. At present (1940) the number of dancers is about 40 to 60. All the dancers are men except three women who "have been initiated" and may join the dance if they desire. In this dance there are men who are dressed like women and imitate women, and others who act like clowns. The dancers form a semicircle and stand in their places as they dance. No drum is used with these songs.

(Catalog No. 2464)

No. 68. "The rain is coming"

Free translation

The clouds and rain are coming

Analysis.—This song begins in major tonality and changes to minor tonality with the same keynote. The repetitions of the song were excellent and the changes in tempo were given clearly.

(Catalog No. 2465)

No. 69. The mockingbird speaks

Free translation

The mockingbird expresses the wish of the dancers for the rain

Analysis.—Beginning in minor tonality, this melody changes to major tonality with the same keynote. It is characterized by a variety of rhythmic phrases, each in a different tempo. This is interesting as the song concerns a mockingbird whose song is varied. Like the other songs of this dance, it has a large compass. Four of these songs have a compass of 11 tones, the present melody has a compass of 12, and the song next following has a compass of 13 tones.

The next was said to be a very old song.

(Catalog No. 2466)

No. 70. Rain dance song

No. 70. Rain dance song—Continued

Analysis.—Like the song next preceding, this begins in minor tonality and changes to major tonality with the same keynote. Several changes in tempo occur in the first portion, but the rhythm of the song as a whole is simple and characterized by 8th and 16th notes.

(Catalog No. 2467)

No. 71. The raingods speak

Free translation

Let us go to the Indian village, said all the raingods,
so that the people of the village will be happy again.

Analysis.—The transcription of this song is from the last portion of the record and was sung twice, the repetition being excellent. There is an urgency in the opening phrase and a pleasing variety in the latter portion. These are interesting in connection with the words. Like the song next following, this contains only the tones of a minor triad and fourth

(Catalog No. 2468)

No. 72. The badger woman speaks

Free translation

Whose will makes all these forests grow?
It is our mother nature makes all these forests grow,
Says the badger woman

Analysis.—The first portion of this song comprises a period of four measures followed by two periods each containing three measures. The second portion is higher, with a different rhythm. The song is minor in tonality, with a compass of 11 tones.

In explanation of the next song it was said that "Rainbow is the name of the spring where the Zuñi worship."

(Catalog No. 2469)

No. 73. At the rainbow spring

Free Translation

At the rainbow spring the dragon-flies start and fly over the rain priests' houses to bring rain to the Indian village. There are blue, red, yellow, white, black and spotted dragon-flies.

Analysis.—The pitch of this song was gradually lowered a whole tone during a few measures, the repeated phrase being sung on the lower pitch, the next phrase raised to the original pitch. These changes are not indicated in the transcription. Margaret Lewis, a Zuñi (cf. pp. 7, 20), was questioned concerning this peculiarity of pueblo singing in 1939 and stated that the Zuñi intentionally raise the pitch level during the songs for rain but in no other class of songs. While her information does not correspond exactly to the song under analysis, it indicates a change of pitch in Zuñi rain dance songs. This is the only Zuñi song of the Rain dance that is major in tonality throughout its length.

Another Rain dance song was recorded but not transcribed, as it contained long passages on a monotone. The words were translated as follows:

On the flower-mountain the clouds will be seen at sunrise, and by noon they will be on our crops, says the sun priest.

CORN-GRINDING SONGS

At Zuñi, as at Santo Domingo Pueblo (cf. Densmore, 1938, pp. 112–118), a distinction is made between the grinding of corn for ceremonial use and that intended for household use. In both pueblos the flutes are played during the grinding of corn for use in ceremonies. The songs here presented are sung during the grinding of corn for household use. This takes place in winter, and it is customary for the women to grind a few days' supply of corn at a time. The women generally work in shifts, 3 or 4 grinding at a time. The women who are grinding the corn may sing as they work, and the women who are waiting their turn may sing while they are waiting. All the corn-grinding songs grow slower at the close, as shown in the transcriptions. The women have charge of the seed corn, as at Santo Domingo, and also of all the corn after it has been brought into the house.

(Catalog No. 2470)

No. 74. Corn-grinding song (a)

Analysis.—The changing tempo of this song may have been due, in part, to circumstances under which the song was recorded. Only the principal changes in tempo are shown in the transcription. The keynote occurs as the opening tone, but appears only as an unaccented tone in the remainder of the song. The melody is pleasing, with a regular rhythm that is probably connected with the motion of grinding the corn. Like the other songs of this series, it ends with a ritard and a phrase in slow tempo.

The next two songs were said to constitute a pair.

(Catalog No. 2471)

No. 75. Corn-grinding song (b)

Voice ♩ = 92
Drum ♩ = 92   Drum in quarter notes

Free Translation

See the clouds coming from the north,
See the clouds coming from the west,
See the clouds coming from the south,
See the clouds coming from the east,
Says the sun priest.

Analysis.—The rhythm of this song resembles that of the song next preceding. The first phrase is four measures in length, with a descending trend of nine tones. The other phrases are generally 6 or 7 measures in length and smaller in compass. The rhythm of the accompaniment is that of the tapping substituted for a drumbeat when the songs were recorded.

(Catalog No. 2472)

No. 76. Corn-grinding song (c)

approximate pitch

Analysis.—This melody contains the regular rhythm of the preceding corn-grinding songs. The pitch was slightly raised in the middle portion, but the pitch was not sustained clearly enough to be indicated in the transcription. The characteristic ending of these songs has been indicated in connection with No. 74.

DANCE SONGS

The Harvest dance is held in the plaza in September. Men do not take part in this dance, both old and young women standing in a straight line and dancing in their places. The singers stand in a group, behind the drum.

The songs of the Harvest and Comanche dances are accompanied by pounding on a typical Pueblo drum which is carried in procession. During the dancing this drum is suspended from a stake, placed upright in the ground (cf. p. 109). Two diagonal notches are made in the stake, the drum being suspended from the upper notch and held in place by a thong around the lower notch.

(Catalog No. 2473)

No. 77. Harvest Dance song

Analysis.—Five renditions of this song were recorded, the transcription being from the first rendition. No differences occur in the renditions except that, in one instance, the closing measures are repeated several times. This is a simple dance song and offers interesting contrasts to the Rain dance and Corn-grinding songs. It has a compass of an octave, like the songs of the Pleasure dance which follow.

The "Pleasure dance" was not described:

(Catalog No. 2474)

No. 78. Pleasure Dance song (a)

Analysis.—Several renditions of this song were recorded and show slight differences in the final phrase. The tones of this phrase are not important, but it was always sung in the indicated tempo, the repetition of the song returning to the original time.

The melody is minor in tonality and the measure lengths are more uniform than in a majority of the songs in this series. The drumbeat was said to be different in this and the next song, but the difference was not audible in the tapping with which the singer accompanied his performance.

(Catalog No. 2475)

No. 79. Pleasure Dance song (b)

Analysis.—The general character of this resembles the preceding dance songs. The rhythm of the opening phrases is repeated on E and D-sharp. A similar phrase at the close of the song contains an interval of a whole tone instead of a semitone. The possibility that the pitch of unimportant tones may be affected by the vowels in the words or accompanying syllables is discussed in the analysis of the following song.

The Comanche tribe were enemies of the Zuñi and invaded their land, but from them the Zuñi obtained the typical Indian dance costume. The Zuñi did not have buckskin until they met the Comanche, but they admired the leather jacket, the feathered war bonnet, and other regalia worn by the Comanche, and adapted the costume to their own use. They also composed songs that were known as "Comanche songs," using them in a dance with that name. An Acoma song of this dance is also presented (No. 40).

The leader of the Comanche dance among the Zuñi is the cacique of the village. The dancers enter the plaza in a group but take the places assigned to them in the dance. They stand side by side in a semicircle, with the drum in the center. The cacique, as leader of the dance, moves inside the semicircle, between the dancers and the drummer whose face is always toward the cacique. The movement is planned in such a manner that the cacique is beside the drummer when the song ends.

The drum is suspended from a notch in a stake which is placed upright in the ground as in the Harvest dance (cf. p. 107). At the close of the dance the drum and stake are carried away.

In this dance there are no singers, the songs being sung by the dancers.

The song next presented was said to be the second song of the dance. The place of the other songs was not designated.

(Catalog No. 2476)

No. 80. Comanche Dance song (a)

Analysis.—In transcribing this song the vowels sung on certain tones were observed closely and it was noted that the vowel with the tone transcribed as D-sharp was *yo*, in which the placing of the voice has a tendency to lower the pitch of the tone. The vowel with the tone transcribed as E was *ee* which does not lower the pitch. In the fourth measure the tone transcribed as D-natural was sung with the vowel *a* which is an open vowel and does not affect the pitch.

(Catalog No. 2477)

No. 81. Comanche dance song (b)

Analysis.—This is an interesting, simple melody in minor tonality, based on the tones of a minor triad. It is the simplest song in the Zuñi series, offering a contrast to the serious songs with which the series opens.

The Deer dance was said to be a "general dance." The song has no words and the singing was accompanied by a notched-stick rattle.

(Catalog No. 2478)

No. 82. Deer dance song

Analysis.—This melody opens with the same count divisions as No. 80, but the first measure is in triple instead of double time.   The form of the melody consists of two periods of 7 measures each, comprising a 2-measure followed by a 5-measure phrase.   The melody is based on a major triad with the keynote midway the compass of the song.

COMPARISON OF THE SONGS OF ACOMA, ISLETA, CO-CHITI, AND ZUÑI PUEBLOS WITH THE SONGS OF CERTAIN OTHER TRIBES [14]

The songs of these pueblos are chiefly major in tonality, 66 percent being in this group (table 1).   The cumulative analysis of 1,553 songs (cf. Densmore, 1939, pp. 35–41) contains only 52 percent in major tonality.   A feeling for the overtones of a fundamental is shown in the relation of the initial tone to the keynote, 65 percent of these songs beginning on the 10th, octave, fifth or third above the key-

[14] Chippewa, Sioux, Ute, Mandan, Hidatsa, Papago, Pawnee, Menominee, Yuman, Yaqui, Nootka, and Quileute.

note, while 28 percent begin on the keynote (table 2). Forty-five percent end on the keynote and 32 percent end on the fifth above the keynote (table 3). This outline of the melodies resembles that of the songs in the cumulative group. In the relation of the entire melody to the final tone, this group differs widely from the large group. The final tone is the lowest tone in only 50 percent of these songs (table 4), while 68 percent of the songs in the large group and on the lowest tone of the compass. The final tone is approached by an ascending progression in only 4 of these Pueblo songs, while the large group contains 184 songs (about 12 percent) with this ending.

In the Pueblo songs, as in the large group, a feeling for the simplest overtones of a fundamental is shown in the compass of the melody, the songs with a compass of an octave constituting 27 percent of the series, while 10 percent have a compass of 10 tones (table 5). The largest compass among the pueblo songs is 11 tones, while the cumulative group contains 23 songs with a compass of 14 and 17 tones. The proportion of songs on the second and fourth 5-toned scales (minor and major pentatonic) is 20 percent in the Pueblo songs (table 6) and 28 percent in the cumulative group.

The general trend in the 1,553 songs comprised in the cumulative analysis is downward, 60 percent of the intervals being descending progressions. This test was applied only to the 40 Acoma songs in which the intervals were counted. It was found that 57 percent of the intervals were descending progressions. In the 82 Pueblo songs under analysis, the descending trend begins with the opening interval more frequently than in the large group, 46 percent of the Pueblo songs having this initial progression (table 7) which occurs in 41 percent of the cumulative series.

The tribes under analysis differ widely in the opening rhythm (meter). Seventy-seven percent of the Pueblo songs begin on the accented part of the measure (table 8), while only 55 percent of the combined group have this beginning. The tribes in the large group vary from 45 percent in the Menominee to 64 percent in the Northern Ute songs with this initial rhythm.

Double time is preferred in the opening measures of these Pueblo songs, 60 percent beginning in 2–4 time (table 9). This opening varies in the cumulative group, in which the highest percentage is 71 in the Yuman and Yaqui songs, and the lowest is 50 percent in the Chippewa songs. A change of measure lengths occurs in 97 percent of these Pueblo songs (table 10) and in only 80 percent of the combined group. The Sioux are next to the Pueblo songs in frequency of a change of measure lengths, 92 percent of the Sioux songs having this varied rhythm. The Pawnee and Yuman and Yaqui are lowest in this respect, only 74 percent in each group having a change of measure lengths.

The percentage of songs containing no rhythmic unit is 50 percent in the Pueblo songs (table 11) and only 30 percent in the combined group. The percentage of songs with one rhythmic unit is only 40 percent in the Pueblo songs and 53 percent in the larger group. The tribes under analysis vary in this respect from 59 percent in the Papago to 72 percent in the Menominee, having one rhythmic unit.

Two peculiarities occurring in Pueblo songs are a change in pitch level during the performance and a structure designated as a period formation. These are considered in the analysis of No. 3, with references to examples in the songs of the present series.

MELODIC AND RHYTHMIC ANALYSES OF ACOMA, ISLETA, COCHITI, AND ZUÑI SONGS BY SERIAL NUMBERS

MELODIC ANALYSIS

TABLE 1.—*Tonality*

	Serial numbers of songs [1]	Number	Percent
Major tonality [2]		54	66
Minor tonality [3]	6, 9, 14, 21, 25, 27, 28, 32, 52, 55, 63, 71, 72, 77, 78, 29, 80, 81.	18	22
Both major and minor, different keynote	38	1	1
Both major and minor, same keynote	68, 69, 70	3	3
Irregular in tonality [4]	5, 12, 15, 22, 24, 66	6	7
Total		82	

[1] Serial numbers are omitted if a group of songs comprises half or more than half the total number.
[2] Songs are thus classified if the third is a major third and the sixth, if present, is a major sixth above the keynote.
[3] Songs are thus classified if the third is a minor third and the sixth, if present, is a minor sixth above the keynote.
[4] Songs are thus classified if the tones are arranged with reference to intervals, without an apparent key note.

TABLE 2.—*First note of song—its relation to keynote* [1]

	Serial numbers of songs	Number	Percent
Beginning on the —			
Tenth	59	1	1
Octave	41, 42, 44, 45, 46, 47, 77, 78, 79	9	10
Sixth	8, 11, 39, 43, 64, 68, 81	7	9
Fifth	1, 3, 9, 13, 16, 19, 20, 23, 26, 29, 30, 33, 34, 35, 36, 40, 51, 53, 57, 58, 60, 67, 76, 82.	24	29
Fourth	61, 70	2	2
Third	14, 18, 21, 38, 63, 65, 69, 71, 75	9	10
Second	37, 80	2	2
Keynote	2, 4, 6, 7, 10, 17, 25, 27, 28, 31, 32, 48, 49, 50, 52, 54, 55, 56, 62, 72, 73, 74.	22	28
Irregular in tonality	5, 12, 15, 22, 24, 66	6	7
Total		82	

[1] Three of these songs (Nos. 19, 37 38) are in 2 sections with different keynotes. This table indicates the relation between the initial tone and the keynote of the first section.

TABLE 3.—*Last note of song—its relation to keynote* [1]

	Serial numbers of songs [1]	Number	Percent
Ending on the—			
Fifth	1, 6, 7, 8, 10, 11, 13, 16, 17, 20, 23, 26, 30, 33, 34, 35, 36, 37, 51, 54, 56, 57, 59, 60, 61, 82.	26	
Third	2, 19, 21, 29, 53, 63, 70, 74, 75, 76, 81	11	13
Keynote	3, 4, 9, 14, 18, 25, 27, 28, 31, 32, 38, 39, 40, 41, 42, 43, 44, 45, 46, 47, 48, 49, 50, 52, 55, 58, 62, 64, 65, 67, 68, 71, 73, 77, 78, 79, 80.	37	45
Pitch uncertain at end	69, 72	2	
Irregular in tonality	5, 12, 15, 22, 24, 66	6	7
Total		82	

[1] Three of these songs (Nos. 19, 37, 38) are in 2 sections with different keynotes. This table indicates the relation between the final tone and the keynote of the final section.

TABLE 4.—*Last note of song—its relation to compass of song*

	Serial numbers of songs	Number	Percent
Songs in which final tone is—			
Lowest tone in song		42	50
Immediately preceded by lower tone and containing lower tones.	21, 36, 40, 55	4	5
Songs containing tones lower than final tone.	1, 4, 11, 12, 15, 16, 17, 19, 22, 23, 24, 29, 30, 31, 33, 38, 39, 41, 42, 43, 44, 45, 46, 47, 52, 58, 61, 62, 63, 66, 67, 70, 81, 82.	34	42
Pitch uncertain at end	69, 70	2	2
Total		82	

TABLE 5.—*Number of tones comprised in compass of song*

	Serial numbers of songs	Number	Percent
13 tones	43, 54, 59, 67, 70	5	5
12 tones	11, 17, 30, 41, 46, 62	6	6
11 tones	14, 24, 29, 38, 45, 47, 55, 56, 64, 68, 71, 73, 76.	13	16
10 tones	2, 19, 21, 22, 39, 42, 44, 49, 53	9	10
9 tones	15, 18, 20, 26, 32, 48, 57, 61, 63, 74, 75	11	12
8 tones	4, 8, 12, 13, 23, 25, 28, 35, 37, 40, 50, 51, 65, 77, 78, 79, 82.	17	27
7 tones	1, 31, 33, 34, 36	5	5
6 tones	6, 7, 9, 10, 16, 27, 52, 58, 60, 80, 81	11	13
5 tones	3, 5, 66	3	3
Pitch uncertain at end	69, 72	2	2
Total		82	

TABLE 6.—*Tone material*

	Serial numbers of songs	Number	Percent
Second 5-toned scale [1]	25, 28, 55	3	3
Fourth 5-toned scale	2, 7, 8, 11, 16, 29, 36, 47, 48, 51, 53, 56, 57, 60.	14	17
Octave complete	33, 39, 61, 63, 67, 68, 73, 74, 75	9	10
Octave complete except 1 tone	1, 4, 9, 13, 17, 18, 20, 23, 26, 27, 30, 31, 32, 34, 35, 42, 43, 46, 49, 62, 64, 70, 76.	23	28
Other combinations of tones	3, 5, 6, 10, 12, 14, 15, 19, 21, 22, 24, 37, 38, 40, 41, 44, 45, 50, 52, 54, 58, 59, 60, 66, 69, 71, 72, 77, 78, 79, 80, 81, 82.	33	40
Total		82	

[1] The 5-toned scales mentioned in this table are the 5 pentatonic scales according to Helmholtz, described by him as follows: "To the second scale, without second or sixth, belong most Scotch airs which have a minor character . . . To the fourth scale, without fourth or seventh, belong most Scotch airs which have the character of a major mode" (Helmholtz, 1885, pp. 260, 261).

TABLE 7.—*First progression—downward and upward*

	Serial numbers of songs	Number	Percent
Downward	2, 3, 7, 8, 10, 11, 13, 14, 15, 17, 19, 21, 29, 37, 38, 39, 41, 42, 44, 45, 46, 47, 51, 61, 64, 64, 65, 66, 67, 69, 72, 74, 77, 78, 79, 80, 81, 82.	38	46
Upward		44	53
Total		82	

RHYTHMIC ANALYSIS

TABLE 8.—*Part of measure on which song begins*

	Serial numbers of songs	Number	Percent
Beginning on unaccented part of measure.	4, 5, 7, 8, 18, 20, 30, 43, 45, 52, 53, 58, 59, 60, 61, 64, 68, 71, 73.	19	23
Beginning on accented part of measure.		63	77
Total		82	

TABLE 9.—*Rhythm (meter) of first measure*

	Serial numbers of songs	Number	Percent
First measure in—2–4 time		50	60
3–4 time	2, 3, 7, 22, 23, 24, 25, 30, 32, 34, 35, 36, 41, 42, 43, 44, 45, 46, 48, 50, 51, 52, 53, 54, 55, 56, 68, 71, 74, 82.	30	37
7–8 time	21, 33	2	2
Total		82	

[1] See footnote 1, table 1.

TABLE 10.—*Change of time (measure lengths)*

	Serial numbers of songs [1]	Number	Percent
Songs containing a change of time		80	97
Songs containing no change of time	6, 20	2	2
Total		82	

[1] See footnote 1, tabe 1.

TABLE 11.—*Rhythmic unit of song*

	Serial numbers of songs [1]	Number	Percent
Songs containing—			
No rhythmic unit		42	50
1 rhythmic unit	1, 3, 6, 9, 12, 18, 20, 21, 28, 30, 31, 32, 35, 36, 38, 40, 41, 48, 50, 51, 52, 54, 55, 57, 61, 64, 81, 82.	28	34
2 rhythmic units	19, 24, 27, 33, 53, 59, 62, 66	9	10
3 rhythmic units	14, 63	2	2
5 rhythmic units		1	1
Total		82	

[1] See footnote 1, table 1.

REFERENCES

BENEDICT, RUTH.
  1931. Tales of the Cochiti Indians. Bur. Amer. Ethnol. Bull. 98.
CULIN, STEWART.
  1907. Games of the North American Indians. 24th Ann. Rep. Bur. Amer.
        Ethnol., 1902–03, pp. 1–846.
DENSMORE, FRANCES.
  1910. Chippewa music. Bur. Amer. Ethnol. Bull. 45.
  1913. Chippewa music—II. Bur. Amer. Ethnol. Bull. 53.
  1918. Teton Sioux muxic. Bur. Amer. Ethnol. Bull 61.
  1922. Northern Ute music. Bur. Amer. Ethnol. Bull. 75.
  1923. Mandan and Hidatsa music. Bur. Amer. Ethnol. Bull. 80.
  1926. Music of the Tule Indians of Panama. Smithsonian Misc. Coll., vol.
        77, No. 11.
  1929 a. Papago music. Bur. Amer. Ethnol. Bull. 90.
  1929 b. Pawnee music. Bur. Amer. Ethnol. Bull. 93.
  1932 a. Menominee music. Bur. Amer. Ethnol. Bull. 102.
  1932 b. Yuman and Yaqui music. Bur. Amer. Ethnol. Bull. 110.
  1932 c. A resemblance between Yuman and Pueblo songs. Amer. Anthrop.,
        vol. 34, No. 4, pp. 694–700. Menasha, Wis.
  1936 a. Cheyenne and Arapaho music. Southwest Mus. Pap. No. 10. Los
        Angeles.
  1936 b. Uses of plants by the Chippewa Indians. 44th Ann. Rep. Bur. Amer.
        Ethnol., 1926–27, pp. 275–397.
  1938. Music of Santo Domingo Pueblo, New Mexico. Southwest Mus. Pap.
        No. 12. Los Angeles.
  1939. Nootka and Quileute music. Bur. Amer. Ethnol. Bull. 124.
  1943 a. Music of Indians of British Columbia. Anthrop. Pap. No. 27, Bur.
        Amer. Ethnol. Bull. 136.
  1943 b. Choctaw music. Anthrop. Pap. No. 28, Bur. Amer. Ethnol. Bull.
        136.
  1956. Seminole music. Bur. Amer. Ethnol. Bull. 161.
  MS. Winnebago Music. Filed Bureau of American Ethnology.
HELMHOLTZ, H. L.
  1885. The sensations of tone. London.
HODGE, FREDERICK WEBB, EDITOR.
  1907, 1910. Handbook of American Indians north of Mexico. Bur. Amer.
        Ethnol. Bull. 30, pts. 1 and 2.
STIRLING, MATTHEW W.
  1942. Origin myth of Acoma and other records. Bur Amer. Ethnol. Bull.
        135.

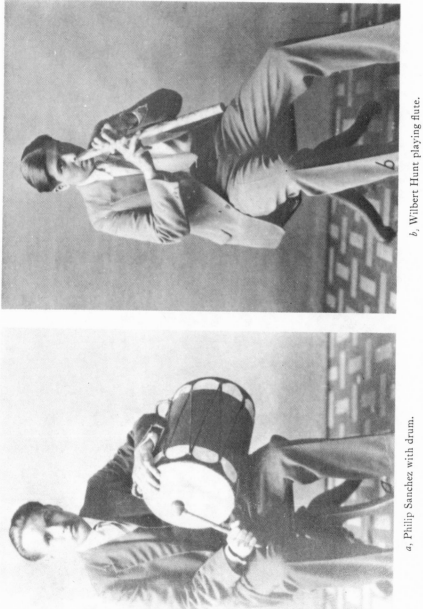

b, Wilbert Hunt playing flute.

a, Philip Sanchez with drum.

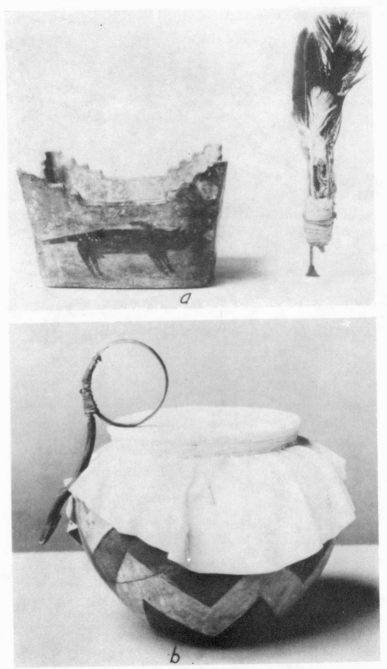

a, Medicine dish and prayer stick.   *b*, Vase drum and drumstick.

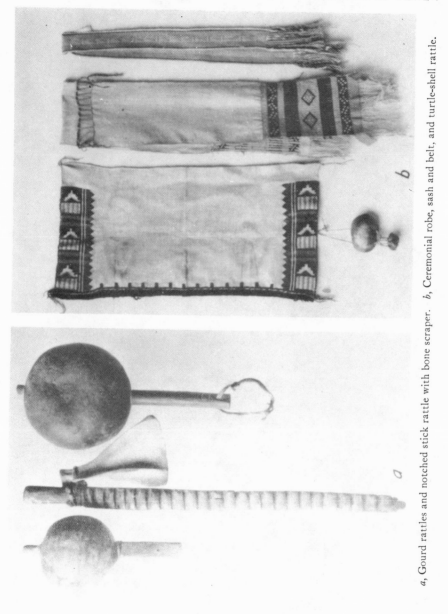

a, Gourd rattles and notched stick rattle with bone scraper. *b*, Ceremonial robe, sash and belt, and turtle-shell rattle.

Replica of headdress worn in Flower Dance, and ring placed on head of woman when carrying jar.

b, Anthony Lucero.

a, Evergreen Tree.

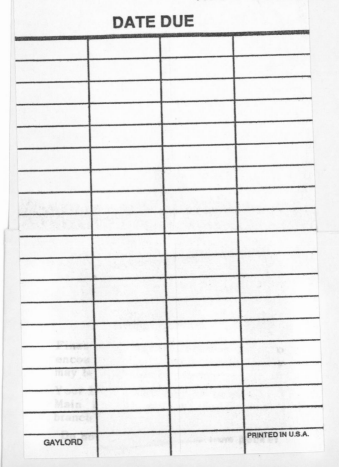